TO LIVE IS CHRIST

A 40-Day Journey with Saint Paul
TO LIVE IS CHRIST

Compiled by Peter Celano

PARACLETE PRESS
BREWSTER, MASSACHUSETTS

To Live is Christ: A 40-day Journey with Saint Paul

2009 First Printing

Copyright © 2009 by Paraclete Press, Inc.

ISBN 978-1-55725-638-6

Unless otherwise noted, all scriptural references are taken from the New Jerusalem Bible, published and copyright © 1985 by Darton, Longman & Todd Ltd. and Doubleday, a division of Random House Inc., and used by permission of the publishers.

Scriptural references from the Psalms and those in the section "Prayers of St. Paul" are taken from the *New Revised Standard Version,* copyright 1989, 1995 by the Division of Christian Education of the National Council of Churches of Christ in the United States of America. Used by permission. All rights reserved.

Scripture quotations that appear in quotations from the Holy Fathers of the last century are retained verbatim as they are given in English translation on the Vatican Web site.

Library of Congress Cataloging-in-Publication Data
Celano, Peter.
 To live is Christ : a 40-day journey with St. Paul / compiled by Peter Celano.
    p. cm.
 Includes bibliographical references (p.   ).
 ISBN 978-1-55725-638-6
1. Bible. N.T. Epistles of Pau—Criticism, interpretation, etc. 2. Paul, the Apostle, Saint. I. Title. BS2650.54.C45 2009
242'.5—dc22   2008048843

10 9 8 7 6 5 4 3 2 1

Published by Paraclete Press
Brewster, Massachusetts
www.paracletepress.com

Printed in the United States of America

CONTENTS

INTRODUCTION

I t has been 2,000 years since the birth of St. Paul, the Apostle to the Gentiles. I would like to begin with the words of Pope Benedict XVI, who established "The Year of St. Paul," asking for special study and recognition of this extraordinary saint. But before I do this, let me suggest how you might use this book in your devotional or study life.

The central focus of *To Live Is Christ* is a series of eight themes, with five points of reflection and study within these themes. Each of these forty reflections features a brief introduction, a portion of Scripture, and a relevant quotation or teaching on that theme from one of the saints, followed by a question to provide you with an opportunity for further reflection.

Before you come to these forty days of reflections on the eight themes, you will have an opportunity to review the stages of St. Paul's life and ministry; this opening section is called "Major Events in St. Paul's Life." Then, following the forty days of reflection is a unique collection of "Prayers of St. Paul" that has never before been published in this format.

You may want to gather a group to study this material together: we have designed the book with that primary purpose in mind. However, if you should choose to discover more about St. Paul by yourself, you will find plenty of guidance along the way.

Here, then, are the words that Pope Benedict XVI used when he asked for this special year of study of the Apostle to the Gentiles:

■

As a model of apostolic commitment, I would like to point to St. Paul in particular, the Apostle of the nations, because this year we are celebrating a special Jubilee dedicated to him. It is the Pauline Year which offers us the opportunity to become familiar with this famous Apostle who received the vocation to proclaim the Gospel to the Gentiles, according to what the Lord had announced to him: "Go, I shall send you far away to the Gentiles" (Acts 22:21). How can we not take the opportunity that this special Jubilee offers to the local Churches, the Christian communities, and the individual faithful to propagate the proclamation of the Gospel to the ends of the world, the power of God for the salvation of everyone who believes (cf. Romans 1:16)?

HUMANITY IS IN NEED OF LIBERATION

Humanity needs to be liberated and redeemed. Creation itself—as St. Paul says—suffers and nurtures the hope that it will share in the freedom of the children of God (cf. Romans 8:19–22). These words are true in today's world too. Creation is suffering. Creation is suffering and waiting for real freedom; it is waiting for a different, better world; it is waiting for "redemption." And deep down it knows that this new world that is awaited supposes a new man; it supposes "children of God."

Let us take a closer look at the situation of today's world. While, on the one hand, the international panorama presents prospects for promising economic and social development, on the other it brings some great concerns to our attention about the very future of man. Violence, in many cases, marks the relations between persons and peoples. Poverty oppresses millions of inhabitants. Discrimination and sometimes even persecution for racial, cultural, and religious reasons drive many people to flee from their own countries in order to seek refuge and protection elsewhere. Technological progress, when it is not aimed at the dignity and good of man or directed toward solidarity-based development, loses its potentiality as a factor of hope, and runs the risk, on the contrary, of increasing already existing imbalances and injustices.

There is, moreover, a constant threat regarding the man-environment relation due to the indiscriminate use of resources, with repercussions on the physical and mental health of human beings. Humanity's future is also put at risk by the attempts on his life, which take on various forms and means.

Before this scenario, "buffeted between hope and anxiety . . . and burdened down with uneasiness" (*Gaudium et Spes*, n. 4), with concern we ask ourselves: *What will become of humanity and creation? Is there hope for the future, or rather, is there a future for humanity? And what will this future be like?* The answer to these questions comes to those of us who believe from the Gospel. Christ is our future, and as I wrote in the Encyclical Letter *Spe Salvi*, his Gospel is a "life-changing" communication that gives hope, throws open the dark door of time and illuminates the future of humanity and the university (cf. n. 2).

St. Paul had understood well that only in Christ can humanity find redemption and hope. Therefore, he perceived that the mission was pressing and urgent to proclaim "the promise of life in Christ Jesus" (2 Timothy 1:1), "our hope" (1 Timothy 1:1), so that all peoples could be co-heirs and co-partners in the promise through the Gospel (cf. Ephesians 3:6). He was aware that without Christ, humanity is "without hope and without God in the world" (Ephesians

2:12)—"without hope because they were without God" (*Spe Salvi*, n. 3). In fact, "anyone who does not know God, even though he may entertain all kinds of hopes, is ultimately without hope, without the great hope that sustains the whole of life" (ibid., n. 27).

THE MISSION IS A QUESTION OF LOVE

It is therefore an urgent duty for everyone to proclaim Christ and his saving message. St. Paul said, "Woe to me if I do not preach it [the Gospel]!" (1 Corinthians 9:16). On the way to Damascus he had experienced and understood that the redemption and the mission are the work of God and his love. Love of Christ led him to travel over the roads of the Roman Empire as a herald, an apostle, a preacher, and a teacher of the Gospel of which he declared himself to be an "ambassador in chains" (Ephesians 6:20). Divine charity made him "all things to all, to save at least some" (1 Corinthians 9:22). By looking at St. Paul's experience, we understand that missionary activity is a response to the love with which God loves us. His love redeems us and prods us to the *missio ad gentes*. It is the spiritual energy that can make the harmony, justice, and communion grow among persons, races, and peoples to which everyone aspires (cf. *Deus Caritas Est*, n. 12). So it is God, who is Love, who leads the Church toward the frontiers of humanity and calls the evangelizers to drink "from the original source, which is Jesus Christ, from whose pierced heart flows the love of God" (*Deus Caritas Est*, n. 7). Only from this source can care, tenderness, compassion, hospitality, availability, and interest in people's problems be drawn, as well as the other virtues necessary for the messengers of the Gospel to leave everything and dedicate themselves completely and unconditionally to spreading the perfume of Christ's charity around the world.

EVANGELIZE ALWAYS

While the first evangelization continues to be necessary and urgent in many regions of the world, today a shortage of clergy and a lack of vocations afflict various Dioceses and Institutes of consecrated life. It is important to reaffirm that even in the presence of growing difficulties, Christ's command to evangelize all peoples continues to be a priority. No reason can justify its slackening or stagnation because "the task of evangelizing all people constitutes the essential mission of the Church" (Paul VI, *Evangelii Nuntiandi*, n. 14). It is a mission that "is still only beginning and we must commit ourselves wholeheartedly to its service" (John Paul II, *Redemptoris Missio*, n. 1). How can we not think here of the Macedonian who appeared to Paul in a dream and cried, "Will you come by to Macedonia to help us?" Today there are countless people who are waiting for the proclamation of the Gospel, those who are thirsting for hope and love. There are so many who let themselves be questioned deeply by this request for aid that rises up from humanity, who leave everything for Christ and transmit faith and love for Him to people! (cf. *Spe Salvi*, n. 8).

WOE TO ME IF I DO NOT PREACH IT!
(1 CORINTHIANS 9:16)

Dear Brothers and Sisters, "*duc in altum*"! Let us set sail in the vast sea of the world and, following Jesus' invitation, let us cast our nets without fear, confident in his constant aid. St. Paul reminds us that to preach the Gospel is no reason to boast (cf. 1 Corinthians 9:16), but rather a duty and a joy.[1]

PART ONE   Major Events in St. Paul's Life

A FIERY PERSONALITY

We don't have a biography of the apostle Paul. None of his contemporaries chose to chronicle his life, and this is somewhat surprising, given its drama, passion, danger, and faith. The Acts of the Apostles tells us many things about Paul, but only in the sketchiest of details.

We also know almost nothing about his physical appearance. This subject has intrigued Christians for 2,000 years, as Paul himself seems to indicate that his appearance was an obstacle throughout his life. In 2 Corinthians chapter 10, he writes: "Look at the evidence of your eyes. . . . For they say, 'His letters are weighty and strong, but his bodily presence is weak, and his speech contemptible' " (vs. 7a, 10).

As for his personality, he must have been fiery. He went from reveling in the persecution of early Christians, to being treated equally roughly by his Jewish brothers after his own conversion. In one instance, for example, Luke writes in the Acts of the Apostles chapter 23, of Paul's being brought to trial before the Sanhedrin—the same group that had tried and sentenced St. Stephen, the first Christian martyr, to death: "Paul looked steadily at the Sanhedrin and began to speak, 'My brothers, to this day I have conducted myself before God with a perfectly clear conscience.' At this the high priest Ananias ordered his attendants to strike him on the mouth" (v. 1–2).

IMPORTANT DATES IN ST. PAUL'S LIFE

Although biblical scholars do not agree on the precise dates of the major events in Paul's life, the following may be their best estimate:

	ca. AD
The Crucifixion of Christ	31–33
Saul's persecutions of the early Christians	33–35
Paul's conversion	35–36
Paul's first visit to Jerusalem	38
Paul's second visit to Jerusalem	46
The first missionary journey	47
Council at Jerusalem, second missionary journey	49
Paul arrives in Corinth	50
First epistles (1 and 2 Thessalonians) written	51
Again in Jerusalem, third missionary journey	52–53
Paul leaves Ephesus	55–56
Again in Jerusalem, arrested at Pentecost	56–57
Paul reaches Rome	59–60
Conclusion of the events told in book of Acts	61
Last epistle written	62
Martyrdom in Rome	64–65

HIS BIRTH AND CHILDHOOD
(date unknown)

We know very little about Paul's childhood, except that he was born as Saul, in the city of Tarsus, a commercial and intellectual center of the Roman Empire, in what is now part of modern-day Turkey. Tarsus was a university town, and two schools of Greek philosophy were centered there: the Stoics and the Epicureans.

Saul was a common name for Jewish boys, usually given in memory of the Saul who was the first king of the ancient kingdom of Israel (cf. 1 Samuel 9–10). As a son in a devout Jewish family, Saul of Tarsus was sent to Jerusalem, probably at about the age of thirteen, to further his studies. There he studied under the renowned Rabbi Gamaliel, also known as Gamaliel the Elder, one of the leaders of the Sanhedrin at that time. Rabbi Gamaliel was the grandson of Hillel, perhaps the most important figure during the entire period known as Second Temple Judaism (from the building of the Second Temple in Jerusalem in 516 BC until its destruction in AD 70).

In Acts 22:3 Paul gives his own testimony:

'I am a Jew,' Paul said, 'and was born at Tarsus in Cilicia. I was brought up here in this city. It was under Gamaliel that I studied and was taught the exact observance of the Law of our ancestors. In fact, I was as full of duty towards God as you all are today.'

It was probably at the conclusion of these studies in Jerusalem that Saul became a Pharisee, a strictly observant, religious Jew.

Paul continues his story in Philippians 3:4–5:

I myself could rely on these [physical qualifications] too. If anyone does claim to rely on them, my claim is better. Circumcised on the eighth day of my life, I was born of the race of Israel, of the tribe of Benjamin, a Hebrew born of Hebrew parents. In the matter of the Law, I was a Pharisee.

PERSECUTOR OF THE FIRST CHRISTIANS (AD 33–35)

Saul was a fierce opponent of the early Christians. As a Jewish religious authority, he zealously persecuted them, fighting for the traditional Jewish faith against the young movement of the disciples of Jesus Christ.

As he says in Acts 22:4,

I even persecuted this Way to the death and sent women as well as men to prison in chains.

He addressed Jesus in Acts 22:20, saying,

When the blood of your witness Stephen was being shed, I, too, was standing by, in full agreement with his murderers, and in charge of their clothes.

In Acts 26:9–11, he described his persecution of the Christians:

I once thought it was my duty to use every means to oppose the name of Jesus the Nazarene. This I did in Jerusalem; I myself threw many of God's holy people into prison, acting on authority from the chief priests, and when they were sentenced to death I cast my vote against them. I often went round the synagogues inflicting penalties, trying in this way to force them to renounce their faith; my fury against them was so extreme that I even pursued them into foreign cities.

Acts 9:1–2 tells of Saul's final trip in search of Christians to persecute:

Saul was still breathing threats to slaughter the Lord's disciples. He went to the high priest and asked for letters addressed to the synagogues in Damascus, that would authorise him to arrest and take to Jerusalem any followers of the Way, men or women, that he might find.

PAUL'S CONVERSION (AD 35–36)

The apostle Paul had one of the most dramatic conversions recorded in all of Scripture. In fact, it was from Saul's experience on the road toward Damascus that we gained the expression "blinded by the light."

Acts 22:6–11

It happened that I was on that journey and nearly at Damascus when in the middle of the day a bright light from heaven suddenly shone round me. I fell to the ground and heard a voice saying, 'Saul, Saul, why are you persecuting me?' I answered, 'Who are you, Lord?' and he said to me, 'I am Jesus the Nazarene, whom you are persecuting.' The people with me saw the light but did not hear the voice which spoke to me. I said, 'What am I to do, Lord?' The Lord answered, 'Get up and go into Damascus, and there you will be told what you have been appointed to do.' Since the light had been so dazzling that I was blind, I got to Damascus only because my companions led me by the hand.

A PRAYER OF ST. JULIAN OF NORWICH

God, of Thy goodness, give me Thyself; for Thou art enough to me, and I can ask nothing that is less that can be full honor to Thee. And if I ask anything that is less, ever shall I be in want, for only in Thee have I all.[2]

SAUL IS BAPTIZED BY ANANIAS, A CHRISTIAN

God spoke to Ananias in Damascus, telling him to find Saul, now blinded as a result of his experience with Christ. At first, Ananias was very afraid.

Acts 9:13–18

But in response, Ananias said, 'Lord, I have heard from many people about this man and all the harm he has been doing to your holy people in Jerusalem. He has come here with a warrant from the chief priests to arrest everybody who invokes your name.' The Lord replied, 'Go, for this man is my chosen instrument to bring my name before gentiles, and kinds and before the people of Israel; I myself will show him how much he must suffer for my name.' Then Ananias went. He entered the house, and laid his hands on Saul and said, 'Brother Saul, I have been sent by the Lord Jesus, who appeared to you on your way here, so that you may recover your sight and be filled with the Holy Spirit.' It was as though scales fell away from his eyes and immediately he was able to see again. So he got up and was baptized.

St. John of Damascus explains:

We confess one baptism for the remission of sins and for life eternal. For baptism declares the Lord's death. We are indeed buried with the Lord through baptism (Colossians 2:12), as St. Paul says. . . . And when the divine Apostle says: "Know ye not, that so many of us as were baptized into Jesus Christ were baptized into his death?" (Romans 6:3), he doesn't mean that the invocation of baptism must be in these words, but that baptism is an image of the death of Christ. . . . He laid on us the command to be born again of water and of the

Spirit, through prayer and invocation, the Holy Spirit drawing nigh unto the water. For since man's nature is twofold, consisting of soul and body, He bestowed on us a twofold purification, of water and of the Spirit: the Spirit renewing that part in us which is after His image and likeness, and the water by the grace of the Spirit cleansing the body from sin and delivering it from corruption, the water indeed expressing the image of death, but the Spirit affording the earnest of life.[3]

ST. JOHN OF DAMASCUS (ca. AD 676–749) was a Syrian monk of the desert and a priest. An Arab Christian, he was known for the beauty of his writing and preaching, and his contemporaries gave him the name "golden speaker."

SAUL—NOW PAUL— BEGINS TO PREACH AND WITNESS FOR CHRIST

After these profound experiences, Saul began using his Roman name, Paulus, or Paul, symbolizing that he was born anew; his Hebrew name, Saul, would no longer suffice. He quickly began doing as God commanded him: preaching.

Acts 26:16

But get up and stand on your feet, for I have appeared to you for this reason: to appoint you as my servant as witness of this vision in which you have seen me, and of others in which I shall appear to you.

Galatians 1:15–17

But when God, who had set me apart from the time when I was in my mother's womb, called me through his grace and chose to reveal his Son in me, so that I should preach him to the gentiles, I was in no hurry to confer with any human being, or to go up to Jerusalem to see those who were already apostles before me. Instead, I went off to Arabia, and later I came back to Damascus.

Acts 9:20–22

He began preaching in the synagogues, 'Jesus is the Son of God.' All his hearers were amazed, and said, 'Surely, this is the man who did such damage in Jerusalem to the people who invoke this name, and who came here for the sole purpose of arresting them to have them tried by the chief priests?' Saul's power increased steadily, and he was able to throw the Jewish colony at Damascus into complete confusion by the way he demonstrated that Jesus was the Christ.

1 Corinthians 9:16

In fact, preaching the gospel gives me nothing to boast of, for I am under compulsion and I should be in trouble if I failed to do it.

> The pope asks us to remember Paul's words:
>
> "Let us set sail in the vast sea of the world and, following Jesus' invitation, let us cast our nets without fear, confident in his constant aid. St. Paul reminds us that to preach the Gospel is no reason to boast, but rather a duty and a joy."
>
> —Pope Benedict XVI[4]

REGRET FOR HIS FORMER LIFE

1 Corinthians 15:9

For I am the least of the apostles and am not really fit to be called an apostle, because I had been persecuting the Church of God.

St. Augustine of Hippo expressed similar regrets about his own pre-conversion life, in some of the most poignant spiritual language we possess—in his famous autobiography, *Confessions*:

Too late have I loved You, O Beauty, ever ancient yet ever new! Too late have I loved You! And look, You were within me and I abroad, and there I searched for You, and, deformed as I was, I pursued the beauties that You have made. You were with me, but I was not with You. Those things kept me far from You, which, unless they were in You, could have had no being.[5]

Galatians 1:21–24

After that I went to places in Syria and Cilicia; and was still unknown by sight to the churches of Judaea which are in Christ, they simply kept hearing it and said, 'The man once so eager to persecute us is now preaching the faith that he used to try to destroy,' and they gave glory to God for me.

From St. Chrysostom's homily on Galatians 1:21–24:

What modesty in thus again mentioning the facts of his persecuting and laying waste the Church, and in thus making infamous his former life, while he passes over the illustrious deeds he was about to achieve! He might have told, had he wished it, all his successes, but he mentions none of these and stepping with one word over a vast expanse, he says merely, "I came into the regions of Syria and Cilicia," and they had heard that he, who once persecuted us, now preaches the faith of which he once made havoc. The purpose of the words "I was unknown to the Churches of Judaea" is to show that so far from preaching to them the necessity of circumcision, he was not known to them even by sight.

ST. JOHN CHRYSOSTOM (AD ca. 347–407) was the archbishop of Constantinople, and was given the Greek surname Chrysostomos by his contemporaries, meaning "golden-mouthed," because of the beauty of his preaching. Churches in both the East and the West honor him as a saint.

NARROW ESCAPE FROM DEATH

Paul was persecuted for his Christian faith—beaten up, imprisoned, held in chains—just as he had once persecuted Christians.

Acts 9:23–25

Some time passed, and the Jews worked out a plot to kill him, but news of it reached Saul. They were keeping watch at the gates day and night in order to kill him, but the disciples took him by night and let him down from the wall, lowering him in a basket.

PAUL GOES UP TO JERUSALEM (AD 38)

Galatians 1:18–24

Only after three years did I go up to Jerusalem to meet Cephas. I stayed fifteen days with him but did not set eyes on any of the rest of the apostles, only James, the Lord's brother. I swear before God that what I have written is the truth. After that I went to places in Syria and Cilicia; and was still unknown by sight to the churches of Judaea which are in Christ, they simply kept hearing it said, 'The man once so eager to persecute us is now preaching the faith that he used to try to destroy,' and they gave glory to God for me.

THE DISCIPLES WERE FIRST CALLED CHRISTIANS (AD 44–45)

At the end of several "missing years" in the life of Paul (we don't know for certain where he was during that time), Barnabas went looking for him, perhaps back in Tarsus. Having found Paul, Barnabas then traveled together with Paul to Antioch. The capital of Syria, Antioch was known as a corrupt and pagan place that the gospel had surely not yet reached. The two men spent a year together there, and the Christian movement to the Gentiles (to *all* people) was born.

Acts 11:26

And when he found him he brought him to Antioch. And it happened that they stayed together in that church a whole year, instructing a large number of people. It was at Antioch that the disciples were first called 'Christians'.

PAUL'S SECOND VISIT TO JERUSALEM (AD 46)

Barnabas and Paul then traveled to Jerusalem to tell the other apostles of their work in Antioch, and to see if the apostles would support them in spreading the gospel far and wide. They received the support that they hoped for, and reassured St. Peter and the other apostles who were taking the gospel to the Jews, that they would never forget "the poor" (see the end of the passage below), meaning the Jewish people, who were usually in poorer circumstances than the Gentiles.

Galatians 2:1–10

It was not until fourteen years had gone by that I travelled up to Jerusalem again, with Barnabas, and I took Titus with me too. My journey was inspired by a revelation and there, in a private session with the recognised leaders, I expounded the whole gospel that I preach to the gentiles, to make quite sure that the efforts I was making and had already made should not be fruitless. Even then, and although Titus, a Greek, was with me, there was no demand that he should be circumcised; but because of some false brothers who had secretly insinuated themselves to spy on the freedom that we have in Christ Jesus, intending to reduce us to slavery—people we did not defer to for one moment, or the truth of the gospel preached to you might have been compromised . . . but those who were recognised as important people—whether they actually were important or not: There is no favouritism with God—those recognised leaders, I am saying, had nothing to add to my message. On the contrary, once they saw that the gospel for the uncircumcised had been entrusted to me, just as to Peter the gospel for the circumcised (for he who empowered Peter's apostolate to the circumcision also empowered mine to the gentiles), and when they acknowledged the grace that had been given to me, then James and Cephas and John, who were the ones recognised as pillars, offered their right hands to Barnabas and to me as a sign of partnership: we were to go to the gentiles and they to the circumcised. They asked nothing more than that we should remember to help the poor, as indeed I was anxious to do in any case.

HIS APOSTOLIC CAREER (AD 47–60)

For about twelve years, Paul traveled all over Asia Minor and parts of what today we call Western Europe, preaching the gospel to the Gentiles. These travels can be described as three primary missions, and their story is told in the Acts of the Apostles: the first mission in Acts 13:1–14:27, the second mission in Acts 15:36–18:22, and the third mission in Acts 18:23–21:17.

CAPTIVITY AND HIS FINAL YEARS
(AD 60–65)

Paul was thrown into jail repeatedly. These occasions gave him the opportunity to share his faith.

Acts 16:23–34

They were given many lashes and then thrown into prison, and the [jailer] was told to keep a close watch on them. So, following such instructions, he threw them into the inner prison and fastened their feet in the stocks.

In the middle of the night Paul and Silas were praying and singing God's praises, while the other prisoners listened. Suddenly there was an earthquake that shook the prison to its foundations. All the doors flew open and the chains fell from all the prisoners.

When the [jailer] woke and saw the doors wide open he drew his sword and was about to commit suicide, presuming that the prisoners had escaped. But Paul shouted at the top of his voice, 'Do yourself no harm; we are all here.' He called for lights, then rushed in, threw himself trembling at the feet of Paul and Silas, and escorted them out, saying, 'Sirs, what must I do to be saved?' They told him, 'Become a believer in the Lord Jesus, and you will be saved, and your household too.' Then they preached the word of the Lord to him and to all his household.

Late as it was, he took them to wash their wounds, and was baptised then and there with all his household. Afterwards he took them into his house and gave them a meal, and the whole household celebrated their conversion to belief in God.

Acts 21:37, 40

Just as Paul was being taken into the fortress, he asked the tribune if he could have a word with him. The tribune said, 'You speak Greek, then?' The man gave his consent and Paul, standing at the top of the steps, raised his hand to the people for silence. A profound silence followed, and he started speaking to them in Hebrew.

On several occasions, he was saved from captivity and death because he was a citizen of the Roman Empire, and on another occasion, because he was exiled. But wherever he was, Paul continued to preach. He exhorted Timothy to follow his example.

2 Timothy 4:1–2

Before God and before Christ Jesus who is to be judge of the living and the dead, I charge you, in the name of his appearing and of his kingdom: proclaim the message and, welcome or unwelcome, insist on it. Refute falsehood, correct error, give encouragement—but do all with patience and with care to instruct.

In his final years, of which we know very little for certain, Paul continued to found churches, possibly in places such as Crete, Spain, Ephesus, and throughout Asia Minor and Macedonia. We know that he yearned to go to Rome. In Acts 19:21 Luke writes: "When all this was over Paul made up his mind to go back to Jerusalem through Macedonia and Achaia. 'After I have been there,' he said, 'I must go on to see Rome as well.'" Paul was martyred in Rome toward the end of the reign of the mad and brutal emperor Nero, probably between AD 64–65.

St. Clement of Rome wrote the following about St. Paul:

By reason of jealousy and strife Paul by his example pointed out the prize of patient endurance. After he had been seven times in bonds, had been driven into exile, had been stoned, had preached in the East and in the West, he won the noble renown which was the reward of his faith, having taught righteousness unto the whole world and having reached the farthest bounds of the West. And when he had borne his testimony before the rulers, so he departed from the world and went unto the holy place, having been found a notable pattern of patient endurance.

ST. CLEMENT was the fourth bishop of Rome, or pope, and the first of the apostolic fathers. This excerpt from his First Epistle, traditionally ascribed to Clement, was written sometime around AD 96 and is one of the oldest Christian documents in existence that is not included in the New Testament.

From the first pope to be honored with the name of "Great":

Our blessed brother, the Apostle Paul, the special teacher of the Gentiles, was associated with Rome at a time when all innocence and freedom was jeopardized under Nero's rule. Nero's fury, which was inflamed by an excess of every vice, hurled him headlong into such a fiery furnace of madness that he was the first to assail Christians with a general persecution, as if God's grace could be quenched by the death of saints. . . . No degree of cruelty could destroy the religion that was founded on the mystery of Christ's cross. Persecution does not diminish but increases the church, and the Lord's field is clothed with an ever richer crop, while the grains, which fall singly, spring up and are multiplied a hundredfold. How large a progeny have sprung from these heaven-sown seeds is shown by the thousands of blessed martyrs who have followed the Apostle's triumphs.

—Pope St. Leo the Great.[6]

PART TWO Forty Days Of Reflection

THEMES FROM
ST. PAUL'S LIFE

THEMES FROM ST. PAUL'S LIFE

St. Paul lived a very large life. He seems, to those of us who have begun to study him, to always have done things wholeheartedly.

As a boy, with a Jewish education, he also studied with some of the greatest rabbis and teachers. As a young man, he didn't simply study the Law or live a faithful, Jewish life, but he also became a Pharisee, a great honor. Then, as a distinguished religious man, he didn't simply study and teach the Torah, but he also became a zealous defender of his faith, to the point of persecuting the first Christians. He was even there when St. Stephen, the first Christian martyr, had his blood shed for following Christ.

Thus far in this book, we have seen what the Bible has to say about these aspects of Paul's life, and more. We have already read about Paul's conversion and baptism, about when he began to preach the Good News, about his trials and imprisonments and escapes, and about his missionary journeys, during which so many of the first church communities were founded. Now we will reflect on some of the themes from his life.

We will explore what conversion really meant to him, and what it means to us. We will look deeper into how and why Paul preached the Gospel, and how we are meant to do the same, in our own ways. We will experience with Paul some of his many trials and afflictions, putting into proper perspective our own troubles and what purposes they may have in a life lived for Christ. And we will discover what it meant to Paul that Jesus appeared before him, and how Jesus is revealed in our lives, today.

Come along, as we take these days to understand the life of St. Paul.

A CONVERTED MAN

Paul's conversion—from being a devout and strictly Orthodox Jew to being a follower of Jesus Christ—was so dramatic mostly because Paul had so very far to go, spiritually speaking. He went from hunting down the followers of Jesus, to becoming not only one of them but also the "Apostle to the Gentiles." Paul always recognized these dramatic contrasts in his encouraging epistles to the early churches, and he saw his conversion as an example of God's tremendous grace.

Acts 22:6–8

It happened that I was on that journey and nearly at Damascus when in the middle of the day a bright light from heaven suddenly shone round me. I fell to the ground and heard a voice saying, "Saul, Saul, why are you persecuting me?" I answered, "Who are you, Lord?" and he said to me, "I am Jesus the Nazarene, whom you are persecuting."

Remembering the Apostle Paul
ST. AUGUSTINE OF HIPPO

The Apostle Paul, being formerly Saul, was changed from a robbing wolf into a meek lamb. He had been an enemy of the Church, but became manifest as an Apostle. Formerly he stalked it, then he preached it. He received from the high priests the authority at large to throw all Christians in chains for execution. "Saul was still breathing threats to slaughter the Lord's disciples" (Acts 9:1). He thirsted for blood, but, "the LORD has them in derision" (Psalm 2:4). When he, having persecuted and vexed in such manner "the Church of God" (1 Corinthians 15:9), Paul came to Damascus and the Lord from Heaven called to him: "Saul, Saul, why are you persecuting me? (Acts 9:5)." I am here, and I am there, I am everywhere: here is My head; there is My body. None of this should surprise us, since we ourselves are members of the Body of Christ. . . .

The Lord directed the Apostle Paul into the things he had to suffer for His Name. He instructed him as to the deeds; He did not stop at the chains, the fetters, the prisons, and shipwrecks; He Himself felt for him in his sufferings, and He guided him towards this day. On a single day we remember the sufferings of both of these Apostles [both St. Peter and St. Paul, on June 29]. Although they suffered on separate days, by the spirit and the closeness of their suffering they constitute one.

Peter went first, Paul followed soon after him. Formerly called Saul, having transformed in himself his pride into humility, he became Paul. His very name, Paulus, means "small, little, less." What is the Apostle Paul after this? Ask him, and he himself gives answer: "I am," he says, "the least of the Apostles. . . . Indeed, I have worked harder than all the others—not I, but the grace of God which is with me" (1 Corinthians 15:9–10).[7]

ST. AUGUSTINE (AD 354–430) is the most important of the Latin Church Fathers. His two books, the *Confessions* and *The City of God*, were two of the most significant books in the first thousand years of Christianity. Like Paul, Augustine was an adult convert to Christianity, and he became the bishop of Hippo, in northern Africa. He wrote many sermons and apologetic writings against the various heresies that were prevalent in those days. This sermon was probably written around the year AD 400, and is used to demonstrate that as early as the late fourth century, Christians were celebrating a joint feast day for Saints Peter and Paul.

REFLECT

Although our experiences of Christ may not have been as dramatic as Paul's was, it is encouraging to cherish and rehearse the moments of transformation that we have experienced. Looking back over your life, at what points in time have you *turned* toward Christ? Where is he asking you to turn today?

Paul "accommodated [him]self to people in all kinds of different situations (1 Corinthians 9:22)" in his effort to reach people of different backgrounds with the message of Christ. He was already a Hebrew, a Roman citizen, and a Greek—with an understanding of Hellenistic culture and philosophy. He used all of these aspects of himself as tools to do the work of spreading the Good News. He saw no shame in emphasizing different aspects of himself, in his preaching and witness. In one instance, for example, he began relating with a group of people simply on the level of sharing the same craft:

Acts 18:1–3

After this Paul left Athens and went to Corinth, where he met a Jew called Aquila whose family came from Pontus. He and his wife Priscilla had recently left Italy because an edict of Claudius had expelled all the Jews from Rome. Paul went to visit them, and when he found they were tentmakers, of the same trade as himself, he lodged with them, and they worked together.

1 Corinthians 9:19–24

So though I was not a slave to any human being, I put myself in slavery to all people, to win as many as I could. To the Jews I made myself as a Jew, to win the Jews; to those under the Law as one under the Law (though I am not), in order to win those under the Law;

to those outside the Law as one outside the Law, though I am not outside the Law but under Christ's law, to win those outside the Law. To the weak, I made myself weak, to win the weak. I accommodated myself to people in all kinds of different situations, so that by all possible means I might bring some to salvation. All this I do for the sake of the gospel, that I may share its benefits with others. Do you not realise that, though all the runners in the stadium take part in the race, only one of them gets the prize? Run like that—to win.

A Leader Should Be Near to His Neighbors Out of Compassion
ST. GREGORY THE GREAT

The pastor should be a near neighbor to every one in sympathy, and exalted above all in contemplation, so that through the depths of loving-kindness he may transfer the infirmities of others to himself, and transcend even himself in his aspiration after the invisible. . . . So it is that St. Paul bends in his compassion upon the secrets of those who are subject to infirmity. In contemplation he transcends heaven, and yet he doesn't desert the troubles of those in need. Being joined at once to the highest and to the lowest by the bond of charity, though in himself caught up in the power of the spirit into the heights above, in his loving-kindness, he reaches others, content to be weak. Hence he says, "If anyone weakens, I am weakened as well; and when anyone is made to fall, I burn in agony myself" (2 Corinthians 11:29). Again he says, "To the Jews I made myself as a Jew" (1 Corinthians 9:20).

He didn't exhibit this behavior by losing hold of his faith, but by extending his loving-kindness—by transferring in a figure the person of unbelievers to himself, to learn from himself how they ought to have compassion shown to them, to the end that he might bestow on them what he would have rightly wished to have had bestowed upon himself, were he as they. Again he says, "If we have been unreasonable, it was for God; if reasonable, for you" (2 Corinthians 5:13). For he had known how both to transcend himself in contemplation, and to accommodate himself to his hearers. . . .

True preachers not only aspire in contemplation to the holy head of the Church, that is to the LORD above, but they also descend in commiseration downward to His members. For this reason, Moses goes frequently in and out of the tabernacle, and he who is wrapped into contemplation within is busied outside with the affairs of those who are subject to infirmity. Within he considers the secret things of GOD; without he carries the burdens of the carnal. And also concerning doubtful matters he always recurs to the tabernacle, to consult the LORD before the ark of the covenant; affording without doubt an example to rulers; that, when in the outside world they are uncertain how to order things, they should return to their own soul as though to the tabernacle, and, as before the ark of the covenant, consult the LORD, if so, they may search within themselves the pages of sacred utterance concerning that whereof they doubt. Similarly, Christ Himself, manifested to us through humility to our humanity, continues in prayer on the mountain, but works miracles in the cities (Luke 6:12), laying down the way to be followed by good rulers: Although already in contemplation aspiring to the highest things, they should mingle in sympathy with the necessities of those in need. True charity rises wonderfully to high things when it is compassionately drawn to the low things of neighbors; and the more kindly it descends to the weak things of this world, the more vigorously it recurs to the things on high.[8]

REFLECT

Paul gives us the example of a converted man who continued to pursue transformation so that he could relate God's loving-kindness to more and more people. Salvation was not enough for him. How have you seen your ongoing Christian conversion, or transformation, become a help in relating to and caring for others around you?

Paul recognized that God's grace had brought him to faith—"I was appointed herald and apostle and . . . a teacher of the gentiles in faith and truth. In every place, then, I want the men to lift their hands up reverently in prayer." (1 Timothy 2:7–8)—and he frequently asked others to join him in praying for God to move in the lives of others.

1 Timothy 2:1–6

I urge then, first of all that petitions, prayers, intercessions and thanksgiving should be offered for everyone, for kings and others in authority, so that we may be able to live peaceful and quiet lives with all devotion and propriety. To do this is right, and acceptable to God our Saviour: he wants everyone to be saved and reach full knowledge of the truth. For there is only one God, and there is only one mediator between God and humanity, himself a human being, Christ Jesus, who offered himself as a ransom for all. This was the witness given at the appointed time.

Pray for the Salvation of Others
POPE PIUS XI

What object could be more worthy of our prayer, and more in keeping with the adorable person of Him who is the only "mediator of God and men, the Man

Jesus Christ" (1 Timothy 2:5), than to beseech Him to preserve on earth faith in one God living and true? Such prayer bears already in itself a part of its answer; for in the very act of prayer a man unites himself with God and, so to speak, keeps alive on earth the idea of God. The man who prays, merely by his humble posture, professes before the world his faith in the Creator and Lord of all things; joined with others in prayer, he recognizes that not only the individual, but human society as a whole has over it a supreme and absolute Lord.

What a spectacle for heaven and earth is not the Church in prayer! For centuries without interruption, from midnight to midnight, is repeated on earth the divine psalmody of the inspired canticles; there is no hour of the day that is not hallowed by its special liturgy; there is no stage of life that has not its part in the thanksgiving, praise, supplication and reparation in common use by the mystical body of Christ, which is the Church. Thus prayer of itself assures the presence of God among men, according to the promise of the divine Redeemer: "Where there are two or three gathered together in my Name, there am I in the midst of them" (Matthew 18:20).[9]

REFLECT

We, too, have been called to pray for, to intercede on behalf of, to give thanks for all people. How do your prayer habits reflect this call? How in your experience does prayer connect you to those who are not living for Christ?

Paul would have known all of the psalms of David by heart. The following psalm speaks profoundly of creation and the law, as paths to having knowledge of God. This sort of "natural" knowledge was a building block for Paul in his conversations with Jewish religious leaders—this was knowledge that he had in common with them.

Psalm 19:1–8
The heavens are telling the glory of God;
    and the firmament proclaims his handiwork.
Day to day pours forth speech,
    and night to night declares knowledge.
There is no speech, nor are there words;
    their voice is not heard;
yet their voice goes out through all the earth,
    and their words to the end of the world.

In the heavens he has set a tent for the sun,
which comes out like a bridegroom from his wedding canopy,
    and like a strong man runs its course with joy.
Its rising is from the end of the heavens,
    and its circuit to the end of them;
    and nothing is hidden from its heat.

The law of the LORD is perfect,
    reviving the soul;
the decrees of the LORD are sure,
    making wise the simple;

the precepts of the LORD are right,
  rejoicing the heart;
the commandment of the LORD is clear,
  enlightening the eyes.

Natural Truth and Revealed Truth
POPE JOHN XXIII

God gave each of us an intellect capable of attaining natural truth. If we adhere to this truth, we adhere to God Himself, the author of truth, the lawgiver and ruler of our lives. But if we reject this truth, whether out of foolishness, neglect, or malice, we turn our backs on the highest good itself and on the very norm for right living.

As we have said, it is possible for us to attain natural truth by virtue of our intellects. But all cannot do this easily; often their efforts will result in a mixture of truth and error. This is particularly the case in matters of religion and sound morals. Moreover, we cannot possibly attain those truths which exceed the capacity of nature and the grasp of reason, unless God enlightens and inspires us. This is why the word of God, "who dwells in light inaccessible" (1 Timothy 6:16), in His great love took pity on man's plight, "became flesh and dwelt among us" (John 1:14), that He might "enlighten every man who cometh into the world" (John 1:9) and lead him not only to full and perfect truth, but to virtue and eternal happiness. All men, therefore, are bound to accept the teaching of the gospel. For if this is rejected, the very foundations of truth, goodness, and civilization are endangered.[10]

REFLECT

Have you discovered the difference between reasoned (natural) knowledge and revealed knowledge? If so, when have you specifically had "revelations" that carried you beyond what you could figure out to what you could know only by faith in the way that Pope John XXIII speaks about?

Paul recognized his sufferings—experienced at the hands of those to whom he was attempting to bring the Good News of Christ—as a participation in the sufferings of Christ. For him all these experiences were just part of a lifelong conversion.

2 Corinthians 1:5–10

For just as the sufferings of Christ overflow into our lives; so too does the encouragement we receive through Christ. So if we have hardships to undergo, this will contribute to your encouragement and your salvation; if we receive encouragement, this is to gain for you the encouragement which enables you to bear with perseverance the same sufferings as we do. So our hope for you is secure in the knowledge that you share the encouragement we receive, no less than the sufferings we bear. So in the hardships we underwent in Asia, we want you to be quite certain, brothers, that we were under extraordinary pressure, beyond our powers of endurance, so that we gave up all hope even of surviving. In fact we were carrying the sentence of death within our own selves, so that we should be forced to trust not in ourselves but in God, who raises the dead. He did save us from such a death and will save us—we are relying on him to do so.

Christ Delivers Us from Death
ST. JOHN CHRYSOSTOM

Paul did not say that God delivers us "from so great *dangers*." He said "from so great a *death*," at once showing the insupportable severity of the trials of Christians who are tried for their faith, and confirming the doctrine of the Resurrection of Christ among us. For even though the Resurrection was a thing of the future, for Paul, at this time, he shows that it happens every day: for when God lifts up a person who is despaired of and has been brought to the very gates of Hades, He shows nothing other than a resurrection, snatching out of the very jaws of death him that had fallen into them. For instance, as in the case of those despaired of and then restored either out of grievous sickness or insupportable trials, it is an ordinary way of speaking to say, "What we have seen, here, is nothing less than a resurrection of the dead."[11]

REFLECT

Where are you experiencing suffering, either physically, or emotionally, or spiritually? Have you asked God to show you how he is using these sufferings to strengthen your life in Christ? How are your sufferings influencing those around you for the good? What has God said to you?

P aul described the purpose of his life to be for preaching the Good News to the Gentiles. "But when God, who had set me apart from the time when I was in my mother's womb, called me through his grace and chose to reveal his Son in me, so that I should preach him to the gentiles. . . ." (Galatians 1:15–16). Gentiles were not simply "non-Jews"; this was also a term that referred to the wider world that had never heard the message of Jesus Christ.

His work seems to have been promised in the following psalm of David:

Psalm 66
Make a joyful noise to God, all the earth;
  sing the glory of his name;
  give to him glorious praise.
Say to God, "How awesome are your deeds!
   Because of your great power, your enemies cringe before you.

All the earth worships you;
  they sing praises to you,
  sing praises to your name."
Come and see what God has done:
  he is awesome in his deeds among mortals.
He turned the sea into dry land;
  they passed through the river on foot.
There we rejoiced in him,
  who rules by his might for ever,
whose eyes keep watch on the nations—
  let the rebellious not exalt themselves.

Bless our God, O peoples,
  let the sound of his praise be heard. . . .

Come and hear, all you who fear God,
  and I will tell what he has done for me.
I cried aloud to him,
  and he was extolled with my tongue.
If I had cherished iniquity in my heart,
  the Lord would not have listened.
But truly God has listened;
  he has given heed to the words of my prayer.

Blessed be God,
  because he has not rejected my prayer
  or removed his steadfast love from me.

Christ to Be Adored by All Nations
THE VENERABLE BEDE

This psalm [Psalm 66] implies the joy of the Lord's Resurrection, not only to the Jews, but also to the Gentiles. Contrary to the persuasion of the Jews, who alleged that they alone of all belonged to the life of blessedness, our Mother, the Church, joyously chants her hope of the General Resurrection, interposing three pauses. In the first portion, she exhorts all men to rejoice together in the Lord's Resurrection, which should bring eternal rewards to all the faithful. "Make a joyful noise to God, all the earth." In the second place, she invites all to come to the contemplation of God's works, that one belief may unite those whom one reward awaits. "Come and see what God has done." Third, she again warns the Gentiles to bless the Lord, Who, though He tries us with various troubles, will yet bring us to the rest of His mercy. "Bless our God, O peoples." In the fourth part, she again invites all, that advised by the example of her deliverance, they may trust the Lord more fully, blessing Him because He has lowered Himself to hear her prayer. "Come and hear, all you who fear God, and I will tell what he has done for me."[12]

THE VENERABLE BEDE (AD ca. 672–735) was known simply as "Bede" throughout his life. An Anglo-Saxon Benedictine monk, he was the most important historian of his day. He is the only Doctor of the Church from Great Britain.

REFLECT

How can you, like St. Paul, give testimony to the call that God placed on your life before you were born? Where can you point to how God has shaped you, even when you were unaware of his hand in the circumstances of your life? How would you explain to someone what that call is—that is, what is your unique role in the kingdom of God?

P aul was at the center of a controversy in the early church, as the apostles tried to discover how to balance their witness to the Jewish people with Paul's new emphasis on reaching beyond the Jewish community to the Gentile nations. As one scholar describes it: "As Jesus incurred the reproach of orthodoxy by his approach to tax collectors, so did Paul by his approach to Gentiles. He saw more clearly than many of his contemporaries the liberating implications of the achievement of Jesus, and the consequent demolition of the barriers separating God from man, and Jew from Gentile."[13]

Galatians 2:7–10

[O]nce [the apostles] saw that the gospel for the uncircumcised had been entrusted to me, just as to Peter the gospel for the circumcised (for he who empowered Peter's apostolate to the circumcision also empowered mine to the gentiles), and when they acknowledged the grace that had been given to me, then James and Cephas and John, who were the ones recognised as pillars, offered their right hands to Barnabas and to me as a sign of partnership: we were to go to the gentiles and they to the circumcised. They asked nothing more than that we should remember to help the poor, as indeed I was anxious to do in any case.

Live and Worship in Unity
ST. IGNATIUS OF ANTIOCH

As children of the light and of the truth, you should shun division and wrong doctrines; and where the shepherd is, there you should follow as sheep. For many specious wolves with baneful delights lead captive the runners in God's race. But where you are as one, they will find no place to hide.

Abstain from noxious herbs, for they are not from the husbandry of Jesus Christ or the planting of the Father. I have not exactly found division among you, but yet I have seen filtering. For as many as are of God and of Jesus Christ, they are with the bishop; and as many as shall repent and enter into the unity of the Church, these also shall be of God, that they may be living after Jesus Christ. Do not be deceived, my brethren. If anyone follows one that makes a schism, he does not inherit the kingdom of God. If anyone walks in strange doctrine, he has no fellowship with the passion of Christ.

Be careful therefore to observe one Eucharist, for there is only one flesh of our Lord Jesus Christ and one cup unto union in His blood. There is one altar, as there is one bishop, together with the presbytery and the deacons my fellow-servants. Whatever you do, may you do it after God.[14]

ST. IGNATIUS OF ANTIOCH (ca. AD 35–110) was a member of the generation immediately following the original apostles. He was born at about the time of St. Paul's conversion. Ignatius was an actual student of St. John, the last living apostle. He wrote several letters as he traveled to Rome, where he knew he would be martyred.

REFLECT

St. Ignatius joins St. Paul in extolling unity and exhorting the followers of Christ to strive for it with all their might. In fact, Paul says that we have unity in Christ, and our job is to protect it. Where, in your thoughts and actions, in your devotional life and in your church life, do you need to work to maintain unity among believers?

Missionaries, as well as those today who strive to live "missionally," have always looked to St. Paul for guidance and advice. We know more about Paul's missionary journeys than about any other person in the Bible. Paul, of course, was looking to the teachings of Jesus for his guidance. Jesus said:

Matthew 10:16–22

Look, I am sending you out like sheep among wolves; so be cunning as snakes and yet innocent as doves. Be prepared for people to hand you over to sanhedrins and scourge you in their synagogues. You will be brought before governors and kings for my sake, as evidence to them and to the gentiles. But when you are handed over, do not worry about how to speak or what to say; what you are to say will be given to you when the time comes, because it is not you who will be speaking; the Spirit of your Father will be speaking in you. Brother will betray brother to death, and a father his child; children will come forward against their parents and have them put to death. You will be universally hated on account of my name; but anyone who stands firm to the end will be saved.

Wolves and Sheep in Those Days
ST. AUGUSTINE OF HIPPO

Consider, my brethren, what Jesus says here. If only one wolf went among many sheep, even if there were several thousands of sheep, all of them would be put to confusion by that one wolf in the midst of them. And though all of them may not be hurt, they would all be frightened. But what sort of advice is this, what sort of counsel, not to let a wolf go among sheep, but to send the sheep against the wolves?! "I send you forth as sheep in the midst of wolves," He says; not into the neighborhood of wolves, but "in the midst of wolves." At that time, there were a lot of wolves and very few sheep. But when the many wolves killed the few sheep, the wolves were changed and became like sheep themselves.[15]

REFLECT

Today in most countries, the wolves are not killing sheep as St. Augustine suggests. Persecution is more subtle. Where in your life, present and past, have you been discriminated against or even hated because of something you were doing for Christ?

Paul offered many words of advice to the first Christians, asking them, above all else, to be witnesses in all aspects of their lives for Christ. Here is one of those words:

Colossians 4:2–6

Be persevering in your prayers and be thankful as you stay awake to pray. Pray for us especially, asking God to throw open a door for us to announce the message and proclaim the mystery of Christ, for the sake of which I am in chains; pray that I may proclaim it as clearly as I ought. Act wisely with outsiders, making the best of the present time. Always talk pleasantly and with a flavour of wit but be sensitive to the kind of answer each one requires.

The Door of the Word Is Opened for You
ST. AMBROSE OF MILAN

Believe the message of the angels: Be lifted up, you everlasting doors, and the King of glory shall come in, the Lord of Sabbath. Your gate is a loud confession made with a faithful voice; it is the door of the Lord, which the Apostle Paul desires to have opened for him. As St. Paul says: That a door of the word may be opened for me, to proclaim the mystery of Christ.[16]

ST. AMBROSE (ca. AD 338–97) was born into a Christian family toward the end of the Roman Empire. He taught rhetoric and worked in local government in Milan, Italy, before becoming the Bishop of Milan. He is probably best known for the role he played in guiding his most famous student, St. Augustine of Hippo, into the Christian Church. Augustine was baptized by Ambrose during the Easter Vigil of 387.

REFLECT

The Spirit opens doors of opportunity for speaking a word for Christ, or for giving a cup of cold water in his name. Where are you standing before an opening door that will give you an opportunity to share the good news of Christ with others?

Paul was always practical, and he insisted on keeping the ultimate purpose of living the Christian life and of doing God's work in focus. As he said to the Corinthians: "Do you not realise that, though all the runners in the stadium take part in the race, only one of them gets the prize? Run like that—to win" (1 Corinthians 9:24).

Romans 15:15–16

But I have special confidence in writing on some points to you, to refresh your memories, because of the grace that was given to me by God. I was given grace to be a minister of Christ Jesus to the gentiles, dedicated to offer them the gospel of God, so that gentiles might become an acceptable offering, sanctified by the Holy Spirit.

The Purpose of the Mission
POPE BENEDICT XVI

The purpose of the mission is that humanity itself becomes a living glorification of God, the true worship that God expects: this is the deepest meaning of *catholicity*—a *catholicity* that has already been given to us, towards which we must constantly start out again. *Catholicity* does not only express a horizontal dimension, the gathering of many people in unity, but also a vertical dimension: it is only by raising our eyes to God, by opening ourselves to him, that we can truly become one.[17]

REFLECT

We have been considering St. Paul's concern that Christians spread the gospel among unbelievers. Here Pope Benedict takes another strand of Paul's message to suggest a larger context of mission. What do you understand to be the meaning of "a living glorification of God"? What are some practical ways that you can keep this "purpose of the mission" in the forefront of your thinking and doing?

TRIALS AND AFFLICTIONS

P aul's life was full of problems—serious ones. In the
following reading, we join a scene in progress, as
Paul is being imprisoned and threatened with physical
violence; and yet, he hears this special message from
Jesus:

Acts 23:10–12

Feeling was running high, and the tribune, afraid
that they would tear Paul to pieces, ordered his troops
to go down and haul him out and bring him into the
fortress. Next night, the Lord appeared to him and said,
'Courage! You have borne witness for me in Jerusalem,
now you must do the same in Rome.' When it was day,
the Jews held a secret meeting at which they made a
vow not to eat or drink until they had killed Paul.

Troubles Are Good for Us
THOMAS À KEMPIS

It is good for us to have trials and troubles at times,
for they often remind us that we are on probation and
ought not to hope in any worldly thing. It is good for

us sometimes to suffer contradiction, to be misjudged by men even though we do well and mean well. These things help us to be humble and shield us from vainglory. When to all outward appearances men give us no credit, when they do not think well of us, then we are more inclined to seek God Who sees our hearts. Therefore, a man ought to root himself so firmly in God that he will not need the consolations of men.

When a man of good will is afflicted, tempted, and tormented by evil thoughts, he realizes clearly that his greatest need is God, without Whom he can do no good. Saddened by his miseries and sufferings, he laments and prays. He wearies of living longer and wishes for death that he might be dissolved and be with Christ. Then he understands fully that perfect security and complete peace cannot be found on earth.[18]

REFLECT

Both St. Paul and Thomas à Kempis say that trials are good for us. How have you experienced trials in the context of "all things working for good" as you have reflected back on them?

Paul's life was constantly in danger, and he spent many days in prison and in religious and civil courts, defending himself and the Lord.

2 Corinthians 4:8–12

We are subjected to every kind of hardship, but never distressed; we see no way out but we never despair; we are pursued but never cut off; knocked down, but still have some life in us; always we carry with us in our body the death of Jesus so that the life of Jesus, too, may be visible in our body. Indeed, while we are still alive, we are continually being handed over to death, for the sake of Jesus, so that the life of Jesus, too, may be visible in our mortal flesh. In us, then, death is at work; in you, life.

In Christ We Are Strong
ST. CATHERINE OF SIENA

We have three chief foes. First, the devil, who is weak if I do not make him strong by consenting to his malice. He loses his strength in the power of the Blood of the humble and spotless Lamb. The world with all its honors and delights, which is our foe, is also weak, save in so far as we strengthen it to hurt us by possessing these things with intemperate love. In the gentleness, humility, poverty, in the shame and disgrace of Christ crucified, this tyrant—the world—is destroyed. Our third foe, our own frailty, was made weak; but reason strengthens it by the union which God has made with our humanity, arraying the Word with our humanity, and by the death of that sweet and loving Word, Christ crucified. So we are strong, and our foes are weak.[19]

> ST. CATHERINE OF SIENA (AD 1347–80) was born Catherine Benincasa, the 24th of 25 children. As a young girl, she defied her parents' wishes by devoting her life to prayer and contemplation rather than to becoming a bride. At sixteen, she became a tertiary of the Dominican Order. St. Catherine is best remembered for her role in encouraging Pope Gregory XI to return the papacy from Avignon, France, back to Rome. She also became a profound theologian and was recognized in 1970 by Pope Paul VI as a "Doctor of the Church."

REFLECT

Using St. Catherine of Siena's outline, how can you remain strong in each of her three categories, even in the midst of your troubles and temptations?

Even after he was stoned by an angry mob, Paul remained committed to his work of spreading the gospel.

Acts 14:19–22

Then some Jews arrived from Antioch and Iconium and turned the people against them. They stoned Paul and dragged him outside the town, thinking he was dead. The disciples came crowding round him but, as they did so, he stood up and went back to the town. The next day he and Barnabas left for Derbe. Having preached the good news in that town and made a considerable number of disciples, they went back through Lystra, Iconium and Antioch. They put fresh heart into the disciples, encouraging them to persevere in the faith, saying, 'We must all experience many hardships before we enter the kingdom of God.'

Freedom in Christ Jesus
TERTULLIAN

Even if you are thrown into prison, you are not, in fact, in prison if you live in the spirit of our Lord. It doesn't matter where you are in the world, if you are without the world. And if you have lost any of the joys of life due to your witness for Christ, this is only good, so that you may gain more than you had before.

If you find yourself in prison, consider that the prison gives to the Christian that which the wilderness did to the Prophets. Also, the Lord Himself often lived in solitude, away from the eyes and approval of other men, so that He might pray more freely, and so that He might withdraw from the world. It was even in a solitary place that He showed His glory to His disciples. Away with the name *prison*! Let us call it a retirement. Though the body be shut up, though the flesh be confined, all is open to the spirit. Roam freely, spirit; walk to and fro, spirit; not setting before you leisurely shady walks, or long cloisters, but the *way* that leads to God. As often as you walk in this way in the spirit, so often will you never be in prison, no matter the outward circumstances. "For wherever your treasure is, there will your heart be too" (Matthew 6:21).[20]

REFLECT

Do you feel confined and limited by circumstances in your life, by physical limitations, by difficult relationships, by "persecution"? What is your prison? How can you take what Tertullian writes and apply it to gain new freedom?

In addition to the major difficulties he faced, Paul struggled with "smaller" afflictions involving his appearance, his physical health, and spiritual matters. Clearly, he knew the power of temptation, and like all of us, he struggled with such things.

1 Corinthians 10:13

None of the trials which have come upon you is more than a human being can stand. You can trust that God will not let you be put to the test beyond your strength, but with any trial will also provide a way out by enabling you to put up with it.

God Will Protect You
THOMAS À KEMPIS

Some people suffer their most serious temptations in the beginning of their conversion, and some at the end. Some are terribly tried their whole life long, while others are only tempted lightly. All of this happens according to the wisdom and justice of the ordering of God, who knows the character and circumstances of each person, and orders all things for the welfare of His people.

Therefore, we shouldn't despair when we are tempted, but fervently we should cry unto God so that He will help us in all our tribulations, and so that He will, as St. Paul says, create a way to escape temptation so that we may be able to bear it. We should all humble ourselves under the mighty hand of God in all temptation and trouble, for He will save and exalt any who are of humble spirit.

A person's character is proven in the midst of temptations and troubles, including what progress he has made, and in progress his reward is great, and his virtues appear. It is not good for a person to be devout and zealous and yet never suffer affliction; but if he behaves himself patiently in the time of adversity, then is there hope of great progress. Some are kept safe from great temptations, but are overtaken in those that are little and common, that the humiliation may teach them not to trust to themselves in great things, being weak in small things.[71]

REFLECT

How do St. Paul's words help you in your present situation? What can you do to be strong during your temptations and troubles?

Paul wanted Christians to understand that faith is a gift, but that remaining faithful is a lifetime commitment.

Romans 15:13

May the God of hope fill you with all joy and peace in your faith, so that in the power of the Holy Spirit you may be rich in hope.

Galatians 5:5–6

We are led by the Spirit to wait in the confident hope of saving justice through faith, since in Christ Jesus it is not being circumcised or being uncircumcised that can effect anything—only faith working through love.

Perseverance in Faith
THE CATECHISM OF THE CATHOLIC CHURCH

Faith is an entirely free gift that God makes to man. We can lose this priceless gift, as St. Paul indicated to St. Timothy: "Wage the good warfare, holding faith and a good conscience. By rejecting conscience, certain persons have made shipwreck of their faith." To live, grow, and persevere in the faith until the end we must nourish it with the word of God; we must beg the Lord to increase our faith; it must be "working through charity," abounding in hope, and rooted in the faith of the Church.[22]

It is easy to become discouraged in the mundane routine of life. What tools do the words of St. Paul and the Catechism give you to help you in persevering?

THE REVELATION OF JESUS CHRIST

Paul saw the Lord appear before him, just as the original twelve disciples had seen him in the flesh.

1 Corinthians 9:1a

Am I not free? Am I not an apostle? Have I not seen Jesus our Lord?

God Reveals Himself
ST. TERESA OF AVILA

It may happen that, very suddenly and in a way that cannot be described, God will reveal a truth that is in Himself and that makes any truth to be found in the world seem like thick darkness. He will also manifest very clearly that He alone is truth and cannot lie. This is a very good explanation of David's meaning in that Psalm where he says that every man is a liar. One should not take those words personally; however, they express an infallible truth. I remember that story about Pilate, who asked Our Lord so many questions, and at the

time of His Passion said to Him: "What is truth?" And
then I reflect how little we understand of this Sovereign
Truth here on earth.[23]

REFLECT

God may not have revealed himself bodily to you, but
write down the ways and the times that you do feel
that God has revealed something of himself to you.

Paul knew that his conversion had nothing to do with his own work or merit, but was due only to God's grace.

1 Corinthians 15:10

But what I am now, I am through the grace of God, and the grace which was given to me has not been wasted. Indeed, I have worked harder than all the others—not I, but the grace of God which is with me.

Turning to God
POPE PIUS XII

With docile [teachable] hearts, then, let all Christians hearken to the voice of their Common Father, who would have them, each and every one, intimately united with him as they approach the altar of God, professing the same faith, obedient to the same law, sharing in the same Sacrifice with a single intention and one sole desire. This is a duty imposed, of course, by the honor due to God. . . . "For we, being many, are one body: all that partake of one bread" (1 Corinthians 10:17).

It is unquestionably the fundamental duty of man to orientate his person and his life towards God. "For He it is to whom we must first be bound, as to an unfailing principle; to whom even our free choice must be directed as to an ultimate objective. It is He, too, whom we lose when carelessly we sin. It is He whom we must recover by our faith and trust" (St. Thomas Aquinas). But man turns properly to God when he acknowledges His Supreme majesty and supreme authority; when he accepts divinely revealed truths with a submissive mind; when he scrupulously obeys divine law, centering in God his every act and aspiration; when he accords, in short, due worship to the One True God by practicing the virtue of religion.

This duty is incumbent, first of all, on men as individuals. But it also binds the whole community of human beings, grouped together by mutual social ties: mankind, too, depends on the sovereign authority of God.[24]

REFLECT

How do you hear God's "voice" in your life? List several specific instances when you knew he "spoke" to you.

Paul was the first and most important witness to the truth of the gospel who had never met Jesus in the flesh. He was not one of the original twelve disciples. As Paul himself said:

Galatians 1:10–12

Whom am I trying to convince now, human beings or God? Am I trying to please human beings? If I were still doing that I should not be a servant of Christ. Now I want to make it quite clear to you, brothers, about the gospel that was preached by me, that it was no human message. It was not from any human being that I received it, and I was not taught it, but it came to me through a revelation of Jesus Christ.

When All Will Be Revealed
ST. AUGUSTINE OF HIPPO

How great will that happiness be, untainted by evil and full of good, when we will have plenty of leisure for praising God! . . . I remember the sacred song, in which we read or hear the words "Blessed are they that dwell in Your house, O Lord; they will be still praising You." All the members of the incorruptible body, which are now busy in various and necessary things, will contribute to these praises. For in that life to come, necessity will have no place; instead, we will have full, certain, secure, and everlasting happiness.

True peace shall be there, where no one will suffer opposition either from himself or any other. God Himself, who is the author of virtue, will be its reward; for, as there is nothing greater or better, He has promised Himself. What else was meant by His word through the prophet, "I will be your God, and you shall be my people" (Leviticus 26:12), than: I will be their satisfaction, I will be all that you honorably desire—life, and health, nourishment and plenty, glory and honor, peace and all good things? This, too, is the right interpretation of the saying of the Apostle Paul: "That God may be all in all" (1 Corinthians 15:28). He will be the end of our desires. He will be seen without end, loved completely, praised without weariness. This outgoing of affection, this pleasure, will certainly be, like eternal life itself, common to all.[25]

REFLECT

St. Augustine gives us here an encouraging picture of our future relationship with Jesus. What do you specifically hope for? What are the differences between how you know God now, and how you will know God in the afterlife?

Perhaps it was because Paul never knew Jesus in the flesh that he came to know him so profoundly in spirit. And the life of the Spirit is not one that is fully revealed. All his life, Paul was very conscious of his imperfections, and of the imperfections of this life compared with the next.

1 Corinthians 13:9–10

For we know only imperfectly, and we prophesy imperfectly; but once perfection comes, all imperfect things will be done away with.

All Will Be Revealed
ST. JOHN OF THE CROSS

When Solomon had completed the building of the Temple, God came down in darkness and filled the Temple so that the children of Israel could not see. Then Solomon said: "The Lord has promised that He will dwell in darkness" (1 Kings 8:12).

The Lord also appeared in darkness to Moses on the Mount, where God was concealed. Whenever God communicated Himself intimately, He appeared in darkness, as may be seen in Job, where scripture says that God spoke with him from the darkness of the air (Job 38:1). All of these mentions of darkness signify the obscurity of the faith when Divinity is concealed, when It communicates Itself to the soul. All of this will be ended when, as St. Paul says, that which is in part shall be ended, which is this darkness of faith, and that which is perfect shall come, which is the Divine light.

Consider the army of Gideon; it is said that all the soldiers had lamps in their hands, but they still could not see because they had the lamps concealed in the darkness of pitchers. Only when the pitchers were broken, was the light seen (Judges 7:19). So faith, which is foreshadowed by those pitchers, contains within itself Divine light, which, when it is ended and broken, at the ending and breaking of this mortal life, will allow the glory and light of the Divinity, which was contained within it, to appear.[26]

REFLECT

Many of the greatest saints, including Mother Teresa of Calcutta, have gone through times of darkness in their relationships with God. How can we find God in the darkness? What are the benefits of this sort of darkness?

The revelation of Jesus Christ is the essence of the Christian message. Paul tells us that the fruit of this revelation is Jesus' reconciling us to himself.

Ephesians 2:14–18

For he is the peace between us, and has made the two into one entity and broken down the barrier which used to keep them apart, by destroying in his own person the hostility, that is, the Law of commandments with its decrees. His purpose in this was, by restoring peace, to create a single New Man out of the two of them, and through the cross, to reconcile them both to God in one Body; in his own person he killed the hostility. He came to bring the good news of peace to you who were far off and peace to those who were near. Through him, then, we both in the one Spirit have free access to the Father.

A Prayer of Pope John XXIII
POPE JOHN XXIII

The sacred liturgy of these days reechoes the same message: "Our Lord Jesus Christ, after His resurrection stood in the midst of His disciples and said: Peace be upon you, alleluia. The disciples rejoiced when they saw the Lord." (Responsory at Matins) It is Christ, therefore, who brought us peace; Christ who bequeathed it to us: "Peace I leave with you: my peace I give unto you: not as the world giveth, do I give unto you" (John 14:27).

Let us, then, pray with all fervor for this peace which our divine Redeemer came to bring us. May He banish from the souls of men whatever might endanger peace. May He transform all men into witnesses of truth, justice, and brotherly love. May He illumine with His light the minds of rulers, so that, besides caring for the proper material welfare of their peoples, they may also guarantee them the fairest gift of peace.

Finally, may Christ inflame the desires of all men to break through the barriers which divide them, to strengthen the bonds of mutual love, to learn to understand one another, and to pardon those who have done them wrong. Through His power and inspiration may all peoples welcome each other to their hearts as brothers, and may the peace they long for ever flower and ever reign among them.[27]

REFLECT

Divisions in the church of God were among St. Paul's greatest concerns. Yet he writes to the Ephesians that God has broken down all separating barriers between peoples. What can you do to promote peace and reconciliation in the world around you?

THEMES FROM
ST. PAUL'S LETTERS

THEMES FROM ST. PAUL'S LETTERS

St. Paul wrote many letters, or epistles, to the fledgling churches that he founded throughout Asia Minor and what we now call Europe. He is traditionally considered the author of more of the New Testament than anyone else except for Luke, who is believed to have written both the Gospel of Luke and the Acts of the Apostles, which together comprise nearly one-third of the entire New Testament.

Paul is described as the author of thirteen letters, or books, of the New Testament. These are:

- Romans
- First Corinthians
- Second Corinthians
- Galatians
- Ephesians
- Philippians
- Colossians
- First Thessalonians
- Second Thessalonians
- First Timothy

- Second Timothy
- Titus
- Philemon

Over the centuries, many people have thought that Paul also wrote the book of Hebrews, but there is not enough evidence for that. Most biblical scholars say that the author of Hebrews will always be a mystery to us.

St. Paul often wrote with the help of a scribe, which means that he would dictate his thoughts and someone else would write them down. Still, there are times when we see Paul himself pick up the pen and say that he was writing a portion, usually at the close of a letter, "with his own hand."

Paul's epistles are full of teachings about how a Christian should live, and the ways in which one may draw close to Christ. As the Venerable James Alberione once said, "The letters of St. Paul are a fountain of good which will vivify all generations. They direct life to its final goal and form apostles. They inflame the heart, fill it with love, and establish all life in charity." Paul actually wrote most or all of his epistles before the four Gospels were written and published. Perhaps this is the reason that he rarely repeats stories from the life of Jesus. Still, we may properly call him the founder of Christian spirituality.

THE GREATEST OF THESE IS LOVE

The spirituality of the early Christians centered on the idea that the temptations and evils of the world may be overcome, and that a Christian life is one that God has transformed in various ways.

Romans 12:1–2

I urge you, then, brothers, remembering the mercies of God, to offer your bodies as a living sacrifice, dedicated and acceptable to God; that is the kind of worship for you, as sensible people. Do not model your behaviour on the contemporary world, but let the renewing of your minds transform you, so that you may discern for yourselves what is the will of God—what is good and acceptable and mature.

True Love Cannot Be Satisfied by Earthly Things
ST. BERNARD OF CLAIRVAUX

The motive for loving God is God Himself. For He is both the efficient cause as well as the final object of our love. He gives the occasion for love, He creates the affection, He brings the desire to good effect. He is such that love to Him is a natural due; and so hope in Him is natural, since our present love would be vain did we not hope to love Him perfectly some day. Our love is prepared and rewarded by His. He loves us first, out of His great tenderness; then we are bound to repay Him with love; and we are permitted to cherish exultant hopes in Him. "He is rich unto all that call upon Him" (Romans 10:12), yet He has no gift for them better than Himself. He gives Himself as prize and reward: He is the refreshment of a holy soul, the ransom of those in captivity. "The Lord is good unto those who wait for Him" (Lamentations 3:25). What will He be then to those who gain His presence?[28]

St. Bernard answered this question in the fourth stanza of his hymn "Jesus, the Very Thought of Thee":

> But what to those who find? Ah, this nor tongue
> nor pen can show; the love of Jesus, what it is, none
> but his loved ones know.

As one whom God loves, describe the joy you have found in knowing God's love personally. If you are God's greatest love, what is *your* greatest love?

Paul's most famous writing comes in the thirteenth chapter of 1 Corinthians, where he articulated the meaning of Christian love.

1 Corinthians 13:1–3

Though I command languages both human and angelic—if I speak without love, I am no more than a gong booming or a cymbal clashing. And though I have the power of prophecy, to penetrate all mysteries and knowledge, and though I have all the faith necessary to move mountains—if I am without love, I am nothing. Though I should give away to the poor all that I possess, and even give up my body to be burned—if I am without love, it will do me no good whatever.

The Incarnate Love of God
POPE BENEDICT XVI

As Saint Paul says, "Because there is one bread, we who are many are one body, for we all partake of the one bread" (1 Corinthians 10:17). Union with Christ is also union with all those to whom he gives himself. I cannot possess Christ just for myself; I can belong to him only in union with all those who have become, or who will become, his own. Communion draws me out of myself towards him, and thus also towards unity with all Christians. We become "one body," completely joined in a single existence. Love of God and love of neighbor are now truly united: God incarnate draws us all to himself. We can thus understand how *agape* also became a term for the Eucharist: there God's own *agape* comes to us bodily, in order to continue his work in us and through us. Only by keeping in mind this Christological and sacramental basis can we correctly understand Jesus' teaching on love. The transition which he makes from the Law and the Prophets to the twofold commandment of love of God and of neighbor, and his grounding the whole life of faith on this central precept, is not simply a matter of morality—something that could exist apart from and alongside faith in Christ and its sacramental re-actualization. Faith, worship and *ethos* are interwoven as a single reality which takes shape in our encounter with God's *agape*. Here the usual contraposition between worship and ethics simply falls apart. "Worship" itself, Eucharistic communion, includes the reality both of being loved and of loving others in turn. A Eucharist which does not pass over into the concrete practice of love is intrinsically fragmented. Conversely . . . the "commandment" of love is only possible because it is more than a requirement. Love can be "commanded" because it has first been given.[29]

REFLECT

How is our love for each other fed by Christ's love for us? Are there specific ways in which Christ loves you that you find it difficult to do for others?

L ove" was often translated as "charity" in centuries past—but both words together capture what a Christian is called to embody in this life.

1 Corinthians 13:4–10

Love is always patient and kind; love is never jealous; love is not boastful or conceited, it is never rude and never seeks its own advantage, it does not take offence or store up grievances. Love does not rejoice at wrongdoing, but finds its joy in the truth. It is always ready to make allowances, to trust, to hope and to endure whatever comes. Love never comes to an end. But if there are prophecies, they will be done away with; if tongues, they will fall silent; and if knowledge, it will be done away with. For we know only imperfectly, and we prophesy imperfectly; but once perfection comes, all imperfect things will be done away with.

The Love Required by God is Intense
ST. JOHN CHRYSOSTOM

How is it possible that one who gives all his goods to feed the poor can be lacking in love? I grant, indeed, that one who is ready to be burned and has the gifts, may perhaps possibly not have love. But one who not only gives his goods, but even distributes them in morsels— how is he not loving? What then are we to say?

Paul's meaning is that those who give should also become joined closely to those to whom they are giving—and not merely to give with sympathy, but in pity and all humility, bowing down and grieving with the needy. For this reason also almsgiving has been enacted by God: since God might have nourished the poor as well without this, but that he might bind us together unto charity and that we might be thoroughly fervent toward each other, he commanded that they should be nourished by us. Therefore, it is said in another place: a good word is better than a gift; and, look, a word is beyond a good gift. Christ Himself says, I will have mercy, and not sacrifice. For since it is common both for men to love those who are benefited by them, and for those who receive benefits to be more kindly affected towards their benefactors, Christ made this law, constituting charity to be a bond of friendship.

But the point remains: How is it that Paul says that those without charity are imperfect? Consider the case of Jesus and the rich man. Jesus said, not merely, "Sell your goods and give to the poor," but He added, "and come, follow Me." Now, not even following Him proves anyone to be a disciple of Christ so completely as does loving one another. For, by this shall all men know, He says, that you are My disciples, if you have love for one another (John 13:35). And also when He says, Whosoever loses his life for My sake, shall find it (Matthew 10:39); and, Whosoever shall confess Me before men, him will I also confess before My Father which is in heaven—by this He does not mean that it is not necessary to have love, but He declares the reward that is laid up for these labors.

Along with martyrdom He requires also this, as He elsewhere strongly intimates, saying, You shall indeed drink of My cup, and be baptized with the baptism that I am baptized with (Matthew 20:23)—that is, you shall be martyrs, you shall be slain for My sake. But to sit on My right hand, and on My left (not as though any sit on the right hand and the left, but meaning the highest precedency and honor) is not Mine to give, He says, but to those for whom it is prepared. Then signifying for whom it is prepared, He calls them and says, Whosoever among you will be chief, let him be servant to you all; in this way He sets forth humility and love.

The love that He requires is intense. Therefore, He did not stop even at this, but added, Even as the Son of Man came not to be ministered unto, but to minister, and to give His life a ransom for many. In this way, He pointed out that we ought to love to the point of being slain for our beloved. For this above all is to love Him.[30]

> THE HOMILIES on First Corinthians are considered the most eloquent of all of St. John Chrysostom's voluminous teachings and sermons.

REFLECT

We are called as Christians to the highest standards of love—to a sacrificial love. What can you do, in your life, to love on those days when you don't feel that the love required of you is possible?

A s we see in the following reading, Jesus connected *love* with *forgiveness*.

Luke 7:36–50

One of the Pharisees invited him to a meal. When he arrived at the Pharisee's house and took his place at table, suddenly a woman came in, who had a bad name in the town. She had heard he was dining with the Pharisee and had brought with her an alabaster jar of ointment. She waited behind him at his feet, weeping, and her tears fell on his feet, and she wiped them away with her hair; then she covered his feet with kisses and anointed them with the ointment.

When the Pharisee who had invited him saw this, he said to himself, 'If this man were a prophet, he would know who this woman is and what sort of person it is who is touching him and what a bad name she has.' Then Jesus took him up and said, 'Simon, I have something to say to you.' He replied, 'Say on, Master.' [Jesus replied,] 'There was once a creditor who had two men in his debt; one owed him five hundred denarii, the other fifty. They were unable to pay, so he let them both off. Which of them will love him more?' Simon answered, 'The one who was let off more, I suppose.' Jesus said, 'You are right.'

Then he turned to the woman and said to Simon, 'You see this woman? I came into your house, and you poured no water over my feet, but she has poured out her tears over my feet and wiped them away with her hair. You gave me no kiss, but she has been covering my feet with kisses ever since I came in. You did not anoint my head with oil, but she has anointed my feet with ointment. For this reason I tell you that her sins, many as they are, have been forgiven her, because she has shown such great love. It is someone who is forgiven little who shows little love.' Then he said to her, 'Your sins are forgiven.'

Those who were with him at table began to say to themselves, 'Who is this man, that even forgives sins?' But he said to the woman, 'Your faith has saved you; go in peace.'

The Difference between Love and Devotion
ST. FRANCIS DE SALES

All true and living devotion presupposes the love of God, and it is neither more nor less than a very real love of God, though not always of the same kind. For the Love that one has shining on the soul we call grace, and makes us acceptable to His Divine Majesty. When it strengthens us to do well, it is called Charity, but when it attains its fullest perfection, in which it not only leads us to do well, but to act carefully, diligently, and promptly, then it is called Devotion. The ostrich never flies, and the hen rises with difficulty, and achieves only a brief and rare flight; but the eagle, the dove, and the swallow are continually on the wing, and soar high: even so, sinners do not rise towards God, for all their movements are earthly and earthbound. Well-meaning people, who have not as yet attained a true devotion, attempt a manner of flight by means of their good actions, but rarely, slowly and heavily. At the same time, really devout persons rise up to God frequently, and with a swift and soaring wing.

In short, devotion is simply a spiritual activity and liveliness by means of which Divine Love works in us, and causes us to work briskly and lovingly; and just as charity leads us to a general practice of all God's Commandments, so devotion leads us to practice them readily and diligently. And therefore, we cannot call one who neglects to observe all God's Commandments either good or devout, because in order to be good, a man must be filled with love, and to be devout, he must further be very ready and apt to perform the deeds of love. And forasmuch as devotion consists in a high degree of real love, it not only makes us ready, active, and diligent in following all God's Commands, but it also excites us to be ready and loving in performing as many good works as possible, even such as are not enjoined upon us, but are only matters of counsel or inspiration.

Even as a man just recovering from illness walks only so far as he is obliged to go, with a slow and weary step, so the converted sinner journeys along as far as God commands him, only slowly and wearily, until he attains a true spirit of devotion, and then, like a sound man, he not only gets along, but he runs and leaps in the way of God's Commands, and hastens gladly along the paths of heavenly counsels and inspirations. The difference between love and devotion is just that which exists between fire and flame—love is a spiritual fire that becomes devotion when it is fanned into a flame. And what devotion adds to the fire of love is the flame that makes it eager, energetic, and diligent, not merely in obeying God's Commandments, but in fulfilling His Divine Counsels and inspirations.[31]

REFLECT

St. Francis de Sales gives practical analogies from nature to help us better understand our Christian "walk." How do you picture your spiritual life moving along the continuum between "journeying slowly and wearily" and "running and leaping"? What can you do to accelerate your pace?

U ltimately, love is about God, not about us or what we do. Our love is made possible only by God's love.

Romans 8:35–39

Can anything cut us off from the love of Christ— can hardships or distress, or persecution, or lack of food and clothing, or threats or violence; as scripture says:

For your sake we are being massacred all day long, treated as sheep to be slaughtered?

No; we come through all these things triumphantly victorious, by the power of him who loved us. For I am certain of this: neither death nor life, nor angels, nor principalities, nothing already in existence and nothing still to come, nor any power, nor the heights nor the depths, nor any created thing whatever, will be able to come between us and the love of God, known to us in Christ Jesus our Lord.

The Prayer Attributed to St. Francis

Lord, make me an instrument of Thy peace;
where there is hatred, let me sow love;
where there is injury, pardon;
where there is doubt, faith;
where there is despair, hope;
where there is darkness, light;
and where there is sadness, joy.

O Divine Master,
grant that I may not so much seek to be consoled,
    as to console;
to be understood, as to understand;
to be loved, as to love;
for it is in giving that we receive,
it is in pardoning that we are pardoned,
and it is in dying that we are born to Eternal Life.
Amen.

REFLECT

Reflect on this prayer each day for the next week. Copy it down and carry it with you. Say it out loud to yourself in the morning before you begin the day.

LIFE IS CHRIST, DEATH IS GAIN

S t. Paul repeats this most important theme over and over again in many different ways in his letters to the early Christians. One might say that this is the essence of the Christian life.

Philippians 1:21

Life to me, of course, is Christ, but then death would be a positive gain.

The Mystery of Human Life Is Unraveled Only in Christ
POPE JOHN PAUL II

Man cannot live without love. He remains a being that is incomprehensible for himself, his life is senseless, if love is not revealed to him, if he does not encounter love, if he does not experience it and make it his own, if he does not participate intimately in it. This, as has already been said, is why Christ the Redeemer "fully reveals man to himself." If we may use the expression, this is the human dimension of the mystery of the Redemption. In this dimension man finds again the greatness, dignity, and value that belong to his humanity. In the mystery of the Redemption man becomes newly "expressed" and, in a way, is newly created. He is newly created! "There is neither Jew nor Greek, there is neither slave nor free, there is neither male nor female; for you are all one in Christ Jesus" (Galatians 3:28). The man who wishes to understand himself thoroughly—and not just in accordance with immediate, partial, often superficial, and even illusory standards and measures of his being— must with his unrest, uncertainty, and even his weakness and sinfulness, with his life and death, draw near to Christ. He must, so to speak, enter into him with all his own self, he must appropriate and assimilate the whole of the reality of the Incarnation and Redemption in order to find himself. If this profound process takes place within him, he then bears fruit not only of adoration of God but also of deep wonder at himself. How precious must man be in the eyes of the Creator, if he "gained so great a Redeemer" (*Exsultet* at the Easter Vigil), and if God gave His only Son in order that man should not perish but have eternal life (cf. John 3:16).

In reality, the name for that deep amazement at man's worth and dignity is the Gospel, that is to say: the Good News. It is also called Christianity.[32]

The two halves of St. Paul's statement in Philippians 1:21 make a whole. Is it possible to believe the first half, without also believing the second half? What does it mean to you to gain by dying?

LIFE IS CHRIST, DEATH IS GAIN

Wmat does it mean to be "raised up to be with Christ"? Paul was always exploring and teaching about these deeper matters of spirituality.

Colossians 3:1–4

Since you have been raised up to be with Christ, you must look for the things that are above, where Christ is, sitting at God's right hand. Let your thoughts be on things above, not on the things that are on the earth, because you have died, and now the life you have is hidden with Christ in God. But when Christ is revealed—and he is your life—you, too, will be revealed with him in glory.

The Presence of the Risen Lord Is Here to Guide Us
POPE LEO THE GREAT

If we unhesitatingly believe with the heart what we profess with the mouth: in Christ we are crucified, we are dead, we are buried, and on the third day, we too are raised. And the hearts of the faithful should know that the Lord promises us His presence as we attempt to spurn the lusts of the world and be lifted by the wisdom from above. The Lord says, "And look, I am with you always; yes, to the end of time" (Matthew 28:20). It was not for nothing that the Holy Spirit said through Isaiah: "The Lord will give you a sign in any case: It is this: the young woman is with child and will give birth to a son whom she will call Immanuel" (Isaiah 7:14). Jesus fulfills the proper meaning of His name, Immanuel, "God with us," and in ascending into the heavens does not forget His adopted brethren. Although he sits at the right hand of the Father, He dwells in the whole body, from above strengthening his people who patiently wait while He summons them upward to His glory.[33]

POPE ST. LEO I was the bishop of Rome from AD 440–61, and the first pope to be given the praiseworthy name of "the Great." He was the first pope to attempt to centralize the authority of the bishop of Rome within Western Christendom. He was widely respected for his spiritual qualities as well as his brilliant preaching. The passage from Paul's Epistle to the Colossians is perhaps the Scripture that he quotes more often than any other in his sermons and letters.

REFLECT

What does it mean for you to live a "resurrected life" here and now? If Christ had not been raised from the dead, our faith would be futile, because we would still be in sin (cf. 1 Corinthians 15:17). But Paul says there is more to the resurrection than our salvation; there is a resurrected living we can do here and now. What would that look like in your life?

P aul taught that we cannot be raised up to be with Christ unless we have also died with him.

Romans 8:12–13

So then, my brothers, we have no obligation to human nature to be dominated by it. If you do live in that way, you are doomed to die; but if by the Spirit you put to death the habits originating in the body, you will have life.

Two Meanings of Death
POPE JOHN PAUL II

Paul's words written to the Romans: "So then, brothers, we are debtors, not to the flesh, to live according to the flesh; for if you live according to the flesh you will die, but if by the Spirit you put to death the deeds of the body you will live" (Romans 8:12–13)—introduce us again into the rich and differentiated sphere of the meanings which the terms "body" and "Spirit" have for him. . . . When he speaks of the necessity of putting to death the deeds of the body with the help of the Spirit, Paul expresses precisely what Christ spoke about in the Sermon on the Mount, appealing to the human heart and exhorting it to control desires, even those expressed in a man's look at a woman for the purpose of satisfying the lust of the flesh. This mastery, or as Paul writes, "putting to death the works of the body with the help of the Spirit," is an indispensable condition of life according to the Spirit, that is, of the life which is an antithesis of the death spoken about in the same context. Life according to the flesh has death as its fruit. That is, it involves as its effect the "death" of the spirit.

So the term "death" does not mean only the death of the body, but also sin, which moral theology will call "mortal." In Romans and Galatians, the Apostle continually widens the horizon of "sin-death," both toward the beginning of human history, and toward its end. Therefore, after listing the multiform works of the flesh, he affirms that "those who do such things shall not inherit the kingdom of God" (Galatians 5:21). Elsewhere he will write with similar firmness: "Be sure of this, that no fornicator or impure man, or one who is covetous (that is, an idolater), has any inheritance in the kingdom of God" (Ephesians 5:5). In this case, too, the works that exclude inheritance in the kingdom of Christ and of God—that is, the works of the flesh—are listed as an example and with general value, although sins against purity in the specific sense are at the top of the list here (cf. Ephesians 5:3–7).[34]

REFLECT

What does it mean to live as one who has died, here in this life? What is God asking you to die to?

Paul was a mystic in many ways. He often spoke of dying in Christ, living in Christ, being resurrected with Christ. These ways of being united with him are at the heart of Pauline spirituality.

Galatians 2:19–20

I have been crucified with Christ and yet I am alive; yet it is no longer I, but Christ living in me. The life that I am now living, subject to the limitation of human nature, I am living in faith, faith in the Son of God who loved me and gave himself for me.

How to Feed Holy Desire
ST. CATHERINE OF SIENA

Perfection is this: that the Word, the Son of God, fed at the table of holy desire for the honor of God and for our salvation; and with this desire He ran with great zeal to the shameful death of the Cross, avoiding neither toil nor labor, not drawing back for the ingratitude and ignorance of us men who did not recognize His benefits, nor for the persecution of the Jews, nor for mockery or insults or criticism of the people, but underwent them all, like our captain and true knight, who was come to teach us His way and rule and doctrine, opening the door with the keys of His precious Blood, shed with ardent love and hatred against sin. As says this sweet, loving

Word, "Look, I have made you a way, and opened the door with My blood. Do not then be negligent to follow it, and do not sit down in self-love, ignorantly failing to know the Way, and presumptuously wishing to choose it after your own fashion, and not after Mine who made it. Rise up then, and follow Me: for no one can go to the Father but by Me. I am the Way and the Door."

Then the soul, enamored and tormented with love, runs to the table of holy desire, and sees not itself in itself, seeking private consolation, spiritual or temporal, but, as one who has wholly destroyed his own will in this light and knowledge, refuses no toil from whatever side it comes. On the contrary, in suffering, in pain, in many assaults from the devil and criticisms from men, it seeks upon the table of the Cross the food of the honor of God and the salvation of men. And it seeks no reward, from God or from fellow-creatures; such men serve God, not for their own joy, and their neighbor not for their own will or profit, but from pure love. They lose themselves, divesting themselves of the old man, their fleshly desires, and array themselves in the new man, Christ sweet Jesus, following Him manfully.

These are the ones who feed at the table of holy desire, and have more zeal for slaying their self-will than for slaying and mortifying the body. They have mortified the body, to be sure, but not as a chief aim, but as the tool which it is, to help in slaying self-will; for one's chief aim ought to be and is to slay the will;

that it may seek and wish nothing other than to follow Christ crucified, seeking the honor and glory of His Name, and the salvation of souls. Such men abide ever in peace and quiet; there are none who can offend them, because they have cast away the thing that gives offense—that is, self-will. All the persecutions which the world and the devil can inflict run away beneath their feet; they stand in the water, made fast to the twigs of eager desire, and are not submerged.

Such a man as this rejoices in everything; he does not make himself a judge of the servants of God, nor of any rational creature; on the contrary, he rejoices in every condition and every type that he sees, saying, "Thanks be to Thee, eternal Father, that Thou hast many mansions in Thy House." And he rejoices more in the different kinds of men that he sees than he would do in seeing them all walk in the same way, for so he sees the greatness of God's goodness more manifest. He joys in everything, and gets from it the fragrance of roses. And even as to a thing which he may expressly see to be sin, he does not pose as a judge, but regards it rather with holy true compassion, saying, "Today it is your turn, and tomorrow mine, unless it be for divine grace which preserves me." [35]

REFLECT

How might you adjust your daily life to feed this holy desire that St. Catherine writes about? What specifically would it cost you to commit yourself to a deeper level of devotions?

To live with Christ, or be in Christ, is to be transformed, says Paul. This doesn't happen all at once: it is a process.

Ephesians 4:20–24

[Y]ou have learnt Christ, unless you failed to hear him properly when you were taught what the truth is in Jesus. You were to put aside your old self, which belongs to your old way of life and is corrupted by following illusory desires. Your mind was to be renewed in spirit so that you could put on the New Man that has been created on God's principles, in the uprightness and holiness of the truth.

How the Soul May Live
ST. TERESA OF AVILA

The silkworm symbolizes the soul that begins to live when, kindled by the Holy Spirit, it begins using the ordinary aids given by God to all, and applies the remedies left by Him in His Church, such as regular confession, religious books, and sermons; these are the cure for a soul dead in its negligence and sins and liable to fall into temptation. Then it comes to life and continues nourishing itself on this food and on devout meditation until it has attained full vigor, which is the essential point, for I attach no importance to the rest.

When the silkworm is full-grown . . . it begins to spin silk and to build the house in which it must die. By this house, when speaking of the soul, I mean Christ. I think I read or heard somewhere, either that our life is hid in Christ, or in God (which means the same thing) or that Christ is our life.[36]

REFLECT

What are the tools of your transformation? St. Teresa talks about sermons, religious books, and regular confession. Are these important to you? Why or why not? What are your other tools for transformation?

M any of the early church communities were in turmoil, fearing for their lives, under threat from the outside; but also, they were sometimes in turmoil within. Paul often counseled them in practical terms on how our life in Christ should change how we behave with each other.

Galatians 5:22–25

On the other hand the fruit of the Spirit is love, joy, peace, patience, kindness, goodness, trustfulness, gentleness and self-control; no law can touch such things as these. All who belong to Christ Jesus have crucified self with all its passions and its desires. Since we are living by the Spirit, let our behaviour be guided by the Spirit.

We Are Restored to Paradise
ST. BASIL THE GREAT

Through the Holy Spirit we are restored to paradise, led back to the Kingdom of heaven, and adopted as children, given confidence to call God "Father" and to share in Christ's grace, called children of light and given a share in eternal glory.[37]

> ST. BASIL OF CAESAREA (AD 330–379), also called "the Great," was a bishop in Cappodocia, part of modern Turkey. A great theologian, he, together with his brother, St. Gregory of Nyssa, and St. Gregory of Nazianzus were known as the Cappadocian Fathers. He authored one of the first written Rules for monastic life, and his feast day is celebrated in both the Eastern and Western Churches.

REFLECT

Local parishes have difficulty living by the fruit of the Spirit; they don't always feel like paradise. Why do you think it is so difficult to live in the Spirit? Which expression of this fruit is most needed in your life at the moment? How can you make yourself more available to receive it?

Might it have been easier to live under the law of Moses than it was for the first Christians to live together as people of one faith in Christ Jesus? Consider these words of St. Paul:

Galatians 3:23–28

But before faith came, we were kept under guard by the Law, locked up to wait for the faith which would eventually be revealed to us. So the Law was serving as a slave to look after us, to lead us to Christ, so that we could be justified by faith. But now that faith has come we are no longer under a slave looking after us; for all of you are the children of God, through faith, in Christ Jesus, since every one of you that has been baptised has been clothed in Christ. There can be neither Jew nor Greek, there can be neither slave nor freeman, there can be neither male nor female—for you are all one in Christ Jesus.

Rediscovering the Mystical Body of Christ, the Church
POPE PAUL VI

The first benefit which We trust the Church will reap from a deepened self-awareness, is a renewed discovery of its vital bond of union with Christ. This is something which is perfectly well known, but it is supremely

important and absolutely essential. It can never be
sufficiently understood, meditated upon, and preached.
What shall We not say about this truth, which is the
principal item, surely, of the whole of our religious
heritage? Fortunately, you already have an excellent
grasp of this doctrine, and here We would add nothing
further except to make a strenuous recommendation
that you always attribute maximum importance to it
and look upon it as a guiding principle both in your
spiritual life and in your preaching of the word of
God.

Consider the words of Our Predecessor, Pius XII,
rather than Our own. In his memorable encyclical
Mystici Corporis he wrote: "We must accustom
ourselves to see Christ Himself in the Church. For it
is indeed Christ who lives in the Church, and through
her teaches, governs, and sanctifies; and it is also Christ
who manifests Himself in manifold guise in the various
members of His society."

How gratifying and pleasant it is to dwell on the
words of Sacred Scripture, the Fathers, Doctors, and
Saints, which come to our minds when we contemplate
this wonderful article of faith. Was it not Jesus Himself
who told us that He was the vine and we the branches?
Do we not have before us all the riches of St. Paul's
teaching, who never ceases to remind us that we "are
all one person in Jesus Christ"? He is always exhorting
us to "grow up in him who is the head, even Christ,

from whom the whole body . . . ," and admonishes us that "Christ is all in all."

As for the Doctors of the Church, We need only recall this passage from St. Augustine: "Let us rejoice and give thanks that we have become not only Christians, but Christ. Do you understand, brothers, the grace of Christ our Head? Wonder at it, rejoice: we have become Christ. For if He is the Head, we are the members; He and we form the whole man . . . the fullness of Christ, therefore; the head and the members. What is the head and the members? Christ and the Church."[38]

REFLECT

From the readings above we learn that we can either live by keeping the law and being right and good, or we can be free to live in Christ. How do you experience these very different ways of living in your life? How can you better live in the Spirit and discover more what it means to have Christ living in you?

A mong the most famous passages from the letters of St. Paul, the following verses speak of faith as a way of growing maturity:

1 Corinthians 13:11–13

When I was a child, I used to talk like a child, and see things as a child does, and think like a child; but now that I have become an adult, I have finished with all childish ways. Now we see only reflections in a mirror, mere riddles, but then we shall be seeing face to face. Now I can know only imperfectly; but then I shall know just as fully as I am myself known. As it is, these remain: faith, hope and love, the three of them; and the greatest of them is love.

Following Christ with Increasing Maturity
MEISTER ECKHART

There are those who walk close by God, at His side, so to speak. They are not wicked, but they are nevertheless immature. For instance, a person may suffer insults, poverty, or physical illness and have no desire to be rid of these things unless God so wills it—but, he would prefer that God should will it. These people do not truly follow Him; instead, they wish to lead God rather than to be led by Him. They would like God to want what they want. Such people run in step with God and at His side. It is true that they want what God wants, but they would prefer God to want what *they* want. . . . In contrast, those who truly follow Him look at nothing behind them and at nothing to one side; they look only to God who is before and above them.[39]

REFLECT

How would you describe in your own words the differences between immature and mature Christians that St. Paul and Meister Eckhart are writing about? Doesn't the first description sound fine, until you read the second one? How do you see your own relationship to God?

The fruit of the spirit does not all come at once in a Christian life; but St. Paul tells us that if we allow God's peace to rule our hearts and Christ to dwell in us, we will bear fruit.

Colossians 3:12–17

As the chosen of God, then, the holy people whom he loves, you are to be clothed in heartfelt compassion, in generosity and humility, gentleness and patience. Bear with one another; forgive each other if one of you has a complaint against another. The Lord has forgiven you; now you must do the same. Over all these clothes, put on love, the perfect bond. And may the peace of Christ reign in your hearts, because it is for this that you were called together in one body. Always be thankful.

Let the Word of Christ, in all its richness, find a home with you. Teach each other, and advise each other, in all wisdom. With gratitude in your hearts sing psalms and hymns and inspired songs to God; and whatever you say or do, let it be in the name of the Lord Jesus, in thanksgiving to God the Father through him.

Advice to One Striving to Do God's Will
ST. PADRE PIO

Regarding what you have asked me, I don't want to say anything more concerning your spirit than this: remain tranquil, striving ever more intensely with divine help to keep humility and charity firm within you, for they are the most important parts of the great building, and all the others depend on them. Keep yourself firmly fixed in them. One is the highest thing, the other the lowest. The preservation of the entire building depends on both the foundations and the roof. If we keep our hearts applied to the constant exercise of these virtues, we will encounter no difficulties with the others. They are the mothers of the virtues; the other virtues follow them like chicks follow their mother.[40]

REFLECT

When in your life is it easiest to be virtuous? What does it mean for you to "put on" virtues and to allow the word of Christ to dwell in you?

Not only does the fruit of the Spirit benefit each individual person, Paul tell us, but also the fruit sustains the whole body of Christ as well.

Romans 12:3–8

And through the grace that I have been given, I say this to every one of you: never pride yourself on being better than you really are, but think of yourself dispassionately, recognising that God has given to each one his measure of faith. Just as each of us has various parts in one body, and the parts do not all have the same function: in the same way, all of us, though there are so many of us, make up one body in Christ, and as different parts we are all joined to one another. Then since the gifts that we have differ according to the grace that was given to each of us: if it is a gift of prophecy, we should prophesy as much as our faith tells us; if it is a gift of practical service, let us devote ourselves to serving; if it is teaching, to teaching; if it is encouraging, to encouraging. When you give, you should give generously from the heart; if you are put in charge, you must be conscientious; if you do works of mercy, let it be because you enjoy doing them.

The Spirit Is One and Undivided in Us
ST. CYRIL OF ALEXANDRIA

All of us who have received one and the same Spirit, that is, the Holy Spirit, are in a sense blended together with one another and with God. For if Christ, together with the Father's and his own Spirit, comes to dwell in each of us, though we are many, still the Spirit is one and undivided. He binds together the spirits of each and every one of us . . . and makes all appear as one in him. For just as the power of Christ's sacred flesh unites those in whom it dwells into one body, I think that in the same way the one and undivided Spirit of God, who dwells in all, leads all into spiritual unity.[41]

> ST. CYRIL OF ALEXANDRIA (AD ca. 378–444) was one of the most influential leaders of the ancient church. He was one of the leading theological voices at the First Ecumenical Church Council of Ephesus in 431. His feast day is celebrated in both the Eastern and Western Churches.

REFLECT

How do you experience the Holy Spirit working among us, between us, in our relationships, and in our parishes?

WITNESSING TO JESUS CHRIST IN OUR LIVES

This final section of our study of St. Paul is where we really put flesh on the bones of his statement that "Life is Christ, death is gain." We die with him; we are raised with him; and then we truly live only when we live with, or in, him.

1 Corinthians 15:21–26

As it was by one man that death came, so through one man has come the resurrection of the dead. Just as all die in Adam, so in Christ all will be brought to life; but all of them in their proper order: Christ the first-fruits, and next, at his coming, those who belong to him. After that will come the end, when he will hand over the kingdom to God the Father, having abolished every principality, every ruling force and power. For he is to be king until he has made his enemies his footstool, and the last of the enemies to be done away with is death, for he has put all things under his feet.

The Resurrection Preached by Paul
POPE JOHN PAUL II

It is difficult to sum up here and comment adequately on the stupendous and ample argumentation of the fifteenth chapter of the First Letter to the Corinthians in all its details. It is significant that, while Christ replied to the Sadducees, who "say that there is no resurrection" (Luke 20:27), with the words reported by the synoptic Gospels, Paul, on his part, replied or rather engaged in polemics (in conformity with his temperament) with those who contested it. In his (pre-paschal) answer, Christ did not refer to his own resurrection, but appealed to the fundamental reality of the Old Testament covenant, to the reality of the living God. The conviction of the possibility of the resurrection is based on this: the living God "is not God of the dead, but of the living" (Mark 12:27). Paul's post-paschal argumentation on the future resurrection referred above all to the reality and the truth of the resurrection of Christ. In fact, he defends this truth even as the foundation of the faith in its integrity: "If Christ has not been raised, then our preaching is in vain and your faith is in vain. . . . But, in fact, Christ has been raised from the dead" (1 Corinthians 15:14, 20).[42]

Why do you think that some of the first-century Gentiles *believed* Paul, when he preached about the Resurrection? How do you find your hope to be based on Christ's resurrection?

The life of faith is fueled by hope. A Christian's job is to remain faithful by being a person of hope. In the following verses, Paul echoes the author of Hebrews 11:1, "Only faith can guarantee the blessings that we hope for, or prove the existence of realities that are unseen":

Romans 8:24–25

In hope, we already have salvation; in hope, not visibly present, or we should not be hoping—nobody goes on hoping for something which is already visible. But having this hope for what we cannot yet see, we are able to wait for it with persevering confidence.

Faith Is Hope
POPE BENEDICT XVI

We must listen a little more closely to the Bible's testimony on hope. "Hope," in fact, is a key word in Biblical faith—so much so that in several passages the words "faith" and "hope" seem interchangeable. Thus the Letter to the Hebrews closely links the "fullness of faith" (10:22) to "the confession of our hope without wavering" (10:23). Likewise, when the First Letter of Peter exhorts Christians to be always ready to give an answer concerning the logos—the meaning and the reason—of their hope (cf. 3:15), "hope" is equivalent to "faith." We see how decisively the self-understanding of the early Christians was shaped by their having received the gift of a trustworthy hope, when we compare the Christian life with life prior to faith, or with the situation of the followers of other religions.

Paul reminds the Ephesians that before their encounter with Christ they were "without hope and without God in the world" (Ephesians 2:12). Of course he knew they had had gods, he knew they had had a religion, but their gods had proved questionable, and no hope emerged from their contradictory myths. Notwithstanding their gods, they were "without God" and consequently found themselves in a dark world, facing a dark future. In *nihil ab nihilo quam cito recidimus* (How quickly we fall back from nothing to nothing.)—so says an epitaph of that period. In this phrase we see in no uncertain terms the point Paul was making. In the same vein he says to the Thessalonians: you must not "grieve as others do who have no hope" (1 Thessalonians 4:13). Here too we see as a distinguishing mark of Christians the fact that they have a future: it is not that they know the details of what awaits them, but they know in general terms that their life will not end in emptiness.

Only when the future is certain as a positive reality does it become possible to live the present as well. So now we can say: Christianity was not only "good news"—the communication of a hitherto unknown content. In our language we would say: the Christian message was not only "informative" but "performative." That means: the Gospel is not merely a communication of things that can be known—it is one that makes things happen and is life-changing. The dark door of time, of the future, has been thrown open. The one who has hope lives differently; the one who hopes has been granted the gift of a new life.[43]

REFLECT

Pope Benedict says, "We see as a distinguishing mark of Christians the fact that they have a future." What do you hope for in your future? What do those around you hope for?

To live in Christ is to live as a resurrection person in a world that Paul describes as longing to be set free.

Romans 8:18–23, 26

In my estimation, all that we suffer in the present time is nothing in comparison with the glory which is destined to be disclosed for us, for the whole creation is waiting with eagerness for the children of God to be revealed. It was not for its own purposes that creation had frustration imposed on it, but for the purposes of him who imposed it—with the intention that the whole creation itself might be freed from its slavery to corruption and brought into the same glorious freedom as the children of God.

We are well aware that the whole creation, until this time, has been groaning in labour pains. And not only that: we too, who have the first-fruits of the Spirit, even we are groaning inside ourselves, waiting with eagerness for our bodies to be set free. . . . And as well as this, the Spirit too comes to help us in our weakness, for, when we do not know how to pray properly, then the Spirit personally makes our petitions for us in groans that cannot be put into words.

Proclaim the Gospel to a World
Longing for Freedom
POPE BENEDICT XVI

We have heard Saint Paul tell us that all creation is even now "groaning" in expectation of that true freedom which is God's gift to his children (Romans 8:21–22), a freedom which enables us to live in conformity to his will. Today let us pray fervently that the Church in America will be renewed in that same Spirit, and sustained in her mission of proclaiming the Gospel to a world that longs for genuine freedom (cf. John 8:32), authentic happiness, and the fulfillment of its deepest aspirations! . . .

Saint Paul speaks . . . of a kind of prayer which arises from the depths of our hearts in sighs too deep for words, in "groanings" (Romans 8:26) inspired by the Spirit. This is a prayer which yearns, in the midst of chastisement, for the fulfillment of God's promises. It is a prayer of unfailing hope, but also one of patient endurance and, often, accompanied by suffering for the truth. Through this prayer, we share in the mystery of Christ's own weakness and suffering, while trusting firmly in the victory of his Cross. With this prayer, may the Church in America embrace ever more fully the way of conversion and fidelity to the demands of the Gospel. And may all

Catholics experience the consolation of hope, and the Spirit's gifts of joy and strength. . . .

"In hope we were saved!" (Romans 8:24). As the Church in the United States gives thanks for the blessings of the past two hundred years, I invite you, your families, and every parish and religious community, to trust in the power of grace to create a future of promise for God's people in this country. I ask you, in the Lord Jesus, to set aside all division and to work with joy to prepare a way for him, in fidelity to his word and in constant conversion to his will. Above all, I urge you to continue to be a leaven of evangelical hope in American society, striving to bring the light and truth of the Gospel to the task of building an ever more just and free world for generations yet to come.[44]

REFLECT

How can you be a resurrection person—one who is, as the pope says, "a leaven of evangelical hope" to those around you? Consider specific ways that you can be that sort of person, today.

The saints are our support, lighting our path. We are able to model ourselves after those, like St. Paul, who show us the way. As St. John Chrysostom said:

> More than anyone else, Paul shows us the nobility of human nature, its capacity for virtue. The greatest force in him was his love for Jesus Christ. With Christ, he believed himself the happiest of people, and without Christ, there was nothing. Threatening mobs and tyrants meant nothing to him. Death was child's play, for all things were to be endured for the only love that mattered."[45]

In fact, Paul asked the Corinthians to look to his example:

1 Corinthians 11:1

Take me as your pattern, just as I take Christ for mine.

The Litany of the Saints (excerpts)
AN ANCIENT CATHOLIC PRAYER

℣. Lord, have mercy upon us.
℟. Christ, have mercy upon us.
℣. Lord, have mercy upon us.

℣. O Christ, hear us.
℟. O Christ, graciously hear us.

℣. O God the Father of heaven.
℟. Have mercy upon us.

℣. O God the Son, Redeemer of the world.
℟. Have mercy upon us.

℣. O God the Holy Ghost.
℟. Have mercy upon us.

℣. O Holy Trinity, one God.
℟. Have mercy upon us.

℣. Holy Mary.
℟. Pray for us.

℣. Holy Mother of God.
℟. Pray for us.

℣. All ye holy Angels and Archangels.
℟. Pray for us.

℣. All ye holy Patriarchs and Prophets.
℟. Pray for us.

℣. Saint Peter.
℟. Pray for us.

℣. Saint Paul.
℟. Pray for us.

℣. All ye holy Apostles and Evangelists.
℟. Pray for us.

℣. All ye holy Disciples of the Lord.
℟. Pray for us.

REFLECT

Are you comforted by praying to the saints? Which saints are your help and guide?

It is important not only to read the epistles of St. Paul but also to put them into practice, finding ways to continue the work of salvation in our own lives.

1 Corinthians 1:18–21

The message of the cross is folly for those who are on the way to ruin, but for those of us who are on the road to salvation it is the power of God. As scripture says: I am going to destroy the wisdom of the wise and bring to nothing the understanding of any who understand. Where are the philosophers? Where are the experts? And where are the debaters of this age? Do you not see how God has shown up human wisdom as folly? Since in the wisdom of God the world was unable to recognise God through wisdom, it was God's own pleasure to save believers through the folly of the gospel.

Continuing the Work of Salvation
POPE BENEDICT XV

It was the desire of Jesus Christ once He had wrought the Redemption of the human race by His death on the altar of the Cross, to lead men to obey His commands and thus win eternal life. To attain this end He used no other means than the voice of His heralds whose work it was to announce to all mankind what they had to believe and do in order to be saved. "It pleased God, by the foolishness of our preaching, to save them that believed." (1 Corinthians 1:21) He chose therefore His Apostles, and after infusing into their minds by the power of the Holy Ghost, the gifts in harmony with their high calling, "Go ye into the world," He told them, "and preach the Gospel." (Mark 16:15) Their preaching renewed the face of the earth. For if the religion of Christ has withdrawn the minds of men from errors of every kind to the truth, and won their hearts from the degradation of vice to the excellence and beauty of every virtue, assuredly it has done so by means of that very preaching. "Faith then cometh by hearing; and hearing by the word of Christ." (Romans 10:17) Wherefore since by God's good pleasure, things are preserved through the same causes by which they were brought into being, it is evident that the preaching of the wisdom taught us by the Christian religion is the means Divinely employed to continue the work of eternal salvation, and that it must with just reason be looked upon as a matter of the greatest and most momentous concern.[46]

BENEDICT XV was pope from 1914 to 1922, throughout the First World War. Physically, he was a small man, but his legacy as a peacemaker, theologian, and healer is enormous. Pope Benedict XVI took his name, Benedict, in part as homage to the life of Pope Benedict XV.

REFLECT

How might you redouble your efforts, now, to continue the work of salvation, as an apostle of the Good News of Christ?

PART THREE Prayers of St. Paul

Prayers of Seeking

"What am I to do, Lord?"
—Acts 22:10a

"Who are you, Lord?"
—Acts 26:15a

O the depth of the riches and wisdom and knowledge of
  God! How unsearchable are his judgments and how
  inscrutable his ways!
"For who has known the mind of the Lord? Or who has
  been his counselor?"
"Or who has given a gift to him, to receive a gift in
  return?"
For from him and through him and to him are all things.
  To him be the glory for ever. Amen.
—Romans 11:33–36

For Thanksgiving in Suffering

Blessed be the God and Father of our Lord Jesus Christ, the Father of mercies and the God of all consolation, who consoles us in all our affliction, so that we may be able to console those who are in any affliction with the consolation with which we ourselves are consoled by God. For just as the sufferings of Christ are abundant for us, so also our consolation is abundant through Christ.

—2 Corinthians 1:3–5

For Strength

For this reason I bow my knees before the Father, from whom every family in heaven and on earth takes its name. I pray that, according to the riches of his glory, he may grant that you may be strengthened in your inner being with power through his Spirit, and that Christ may dwell in your hearts through faith, as you are being rooted and grounded in love. I pray that you may have the power to comprehend, with all the saints, what is the breadth and length and height and depth, and to know the love of Christ that surpasses knowledge, so that you may be filled with all the fullness of God. Now to him who by the power at work within us is able to accomplish abundantly far more than all we can ask or imagine, to him be glory in the church and in Christ Jesus to all generations, for ever and ever. Amen.

—Ephesians 3:14–21

May you be made strong with all the strength that comes from his glorious power, and may you be prepared to endure everything with patience, while joyfully giving thanks to the Father, who has enabled you to share in the inheritance of the saints in the light. He has rescued us from the power of darkness and transferred us into the kingdom of his beloved Son, in whom we have redemption, the forgiveness of sins.

—Colossians 1:11–14

In Praise of God's Power and Presence

In the presence of God, who gives life to all things, and of Christ Jesus . . . who is the blessed and only Sovereign, the King of kings and Lord of lords. It is he alone who has immortality and dwells in unapproachable light, whom no one has ever seen or can see; to him be honor and eternal dominion. Amen.

—1 Timothy 6:13, 15–16

Simple Prayers of Faith

I can do all things through him who strengthens me.
—Philippians 4:13

And my God will fully satisfy every need of yours according to his riches in glory in Christ Jesus. To our God and Father be glory for ever and ever. Amen.
—Philippians 4:19–20

God knows.
—2 Corinthians 12:2, 3

St. Paul's Prayer for You

I bow my knees before the Father. . . . I pray that, according to the riches of his glory, he may grant that you may be strengthened in your inner being with power through his Spirit, and that Christ may dwell in your hearts through faith, as you are being rooted and grounded in love. I pray that you may have the power to comprehend, with all the saints, what is the breadth and length and height and depth, and to know the love of Christ that surpasses knowledge, so that you may be filled with all the fullness of God.

—Ephesians 3:14, 16–19

NOTES

1. Message of His Holiness Benedict XVI for the eighty-second World Mission Sunday 2008, from the Vatican, May 11, 2008.

2. Julian of Norwich, *Revelations*, in *The Complete Julian*, trans. Fr. John-Julian (Brewster, MA: Paraclete Press, 2009).

3. St. John of Damascus, *An Exposition of the Orthodox Faith*, Book IV, chapter 9. All translations are the editor's, unless otherwise noted.

4. Message of His Holiness Benedict XVI for the eighty-second World Mission Sunday 2008, from the Vatican, May 11, 2008.

5. St. Augustine, *Confessions*, Book X, chapter xxvii.

6. Pope Leo the Great's Sermon LXXXII, "On the Feast of the Apostles Peter and Paul," paragraph 6.

7. Extract from Augustine's famous sermon on Sts. Peter and Paul.

8. St. Gregory the Great, *Pastoral Care*, chapter 5.

9. *Caritate Christi Compulsi*, the Encyclical of Pope Pius XI on the Sacred Heart, May 3, 1932; paragraphs 16–17.

10. *Ad Petri Cathedram*, the Encyclical of Pope John XXIII on Truth, Unity, and Peace, in a Spirit of Charity, June 29, 1959; paragraphs 6–8.

11. Extract from John Chrysostom's Second Homily on Second Corinthians.

12. Quoted in John Mason Neale, *A Commentary on the Psalms: From Primitive and Medieval Writers*, vol. 2 (New York: Pott and Amery, 1868), 312.

13. F.F. Bruce, in back cover endorsement to Gunther Bornkamm's book *Paul* (New York: Harper & Row, 1971).

14. St. Ignatius of Antioch, *Letter to the Philadelphians*, chapters 2–4.

15. St. Augustine, Sermon XIV, originally delivered on a Festival of Martyrs; paragraph 1.

16. St. Ambrose of Milan, *Exposition of the Christian Faith*, Book IV, paragraph 21.

17. Pope Benedict XVI, Homily on the Solemnity of Sts. Peter and Paul, June 29, 2005; paragraph 2.

18. Thomas à Kempis, *The Imitation of Christ*, Book I, chapter 12.

19. From a letter to Queen Giovanna of Naples, taken from *Saint Catherine of Siena as Seen in Her Letters*, trans. and ed. Vida D. Scudder (New York: E.P. Dutton, 1905).

20. Tertullian, "An Address to the Martyrs," paragraph 2.

21. Thomas à Kempis, *The Imitation of Christ*, Book I, chapter 13.

22. The *Catechism of the Catholic Church*, paragraph 162.

23. St. Teresa of Avila, *Interior Castle*, part VI, chapter 10.

24. *Mediator Dei*, the Encyclical of Pope Pius XII on The Sacred Liturgy, November 20, 1947; paragraphs 12–14.

25. St. Augustine, *The City of God*, Book XXII, chapter 30.

26. St. John of the Cross, *The Ascent of Mount Carmel*, chapter 9, paragraph 3.

27. *Pacem in Terris*, the Encyclical of Pope John XXIII, April 11, 1963; paragraphs 170–71.

28. St. Bernard of Clairaux, *On Loving God*, chapter 7.

29. *Deus Caritas Est*, the Encyclical of Pope Benedict XVI, December 25, 2005; paragraph 14.

30. Extract from St. Chrysostom's Homily 32 on First Corinthians.

31. St. Francis de Sales, *Introduction to the Devout Life*, chapter 1.

32. *Redemptor Hominis*, the Encyclical of Pope John Paul II, March 4, 1979; paragraph 10.

33. Pope Leo the Great's Sermon LXXII, "On the Lord's Resurrection, II," paragraph 3.

34. *L'Osservatore Romano*, Weekly Edition in English, January 12, 1981.

35. From a letter to Brother William of England, taken from *Saint Catherine of Siena as Seen in Her Letters,* trans. and ed. Vida D. Scudder.

36. St. Teresa of Avila, *The Interior Castle*, chapter 2.

37. Quoted in the *Catechism of the Catholic Church*, paragraph 736.

38. Encyclical of Pope Paul VI on the Church, August 6, 1964; paragraph 35.

39. Meister Eckhart's famous sermon "Sequere Me" (preached on John 1:43); paragraphs 6 and 8.

40. Padre Pio, *Words of Light: Inspiration from the Letters of Padre Pio*, trans. Fr. Raniero Cantalamessa (Brewster, MA: Paraclete Press, 2008), 166–67.

41. Quoted in the *Catechism of the Catholic Church*, paragraph 738.

42. *L'Osservatore Romano*, Weekly Edition in English, February 1, 1982.

43. *Spe Salvi*, the Encyclical of Pope Benedict XVI, November 30, 2007; paragraph 2.

44. From a sermon of His Holiness Pope Benedict XVI, preached at Washington Nationals' Stadium, April 17, 2008.

45. St. John Chrysostom's "Second Sermon in Praise of St. Paul"; extracts.

46. *Humani Generis Redemptionem*, the Encyclical of Pope Benedict XV, on Preaching the Word of God, June 15, 1917.